T0312777

Computing Networks

Computing Networks

from cluster to cloud computing

Pascale Vicat-Blanc
Sébastien Soudan
Romaric Guillier
Brice Goglin

First published 2011 in Great Britain and the United States by ISTE Ltd and John Wiley & Sons, Inc.

ISTE Ltd
27-37 St George's Road
London SW19 4EU
UK

www.iste.co.uk

John Wiley & Sons, Inc.
111 River Street
Hoboken, NJ 07030
USA

www.wiley.com

© ISTE Ltd 2011

Library of Congress Cataloging-in-Publication Data

Reseaux de calcul. English
  Computing networks : from cluster to cloud computing / Pascale Vicat-Blanc ... [et al.].
    p. cm.
  Includes bibliographical references and index.
  ISBN 978-1-84821-286-2
  1. Computer networks. I. Vicat-Blanc, Pascale. II. Title.
  TK5105.5.R448613 2011
  004.6--dc22

                                                                      2011006658

British Library Cataloguing-in-Publication Data
A CIP record for this book is available from the British Library
ISBN 978-1-84821-286-2

Printed and bound in Great Britain by CPI Antony Rowe, Chippenham and Eastbourne.

Table of Contents

Introduction

Since the advent of the computer in 1940, computing power needs have not ceased to increase. Today, great scientific fields such as high-energy physics, astrophysics, climatology, biology and medical imagery rely on new mutualization technologies and worldwide sharing of computer potential across international grids to meet the huge demand for data processing. Every day, researchers submit hundreds of computations to large-scale distributed infrastructures such as the European Enabling Grids for E-sciencE grid (EGEE) [EGE 04], which gathers more than 100,000 processors. Soon European Grid Infrastructure (EGI) and TeraGrid [PRO 11] in the United States will each be able to aggregate more than double this number of processors. In the near future many industrial domains, such as automobile, energy and transport, which are increasingly relying on digital simulation, will be able to benefit from large shared reservoirs of computer resources. This approach will shortly be extended to e-commerce, finance and the leisure industry.

Over the past 15 years, three key technologies have followed each other in response to this growing computing power demand. These technologies embody the revolution of network computing: computer clusters, computing grids and computing clouds. A quick definition of these is as follows:

– a computing cluster is a collection of PCs interconnected via local-area, very-low-latency, high-speed networks;

– a computing grid is the aggregation of a very large number of distributed computing and storage resources, interconnected via wide-area networks. There are computing grids dedicated to intensive computations of data grids that store, process and give access to massive amounts of data in the order of hundreds of gigabytes or even several terabytes;

– a computing cloud provides access services to resources via the Internet. The underlying infrastructure is totally concealed from users. The available resources are generally virtual machines housed in resource centers, also called data centers.

Originally, it was the spectacular advances in transmission and communication technologies that enabled researchers to imagine these distributed architectures. These technologies made the aggregation and mutualization of computer equipment possible, which led to the rise in power of global computing. The hardware and software of interconnection networks, which are transparent in appearance, play a complex role that is difficult to grasp and not often studied. Yet the place of the network is central and its evolution will certainly be a key to ubiquitous computer systems to come.

Indeed, to make full use of a mutualized communication network, sharing policies implemented by robust and scalable arbitration and orchestration mechanisms are necessary. Today these mechanisms are included in distributed software called communication protocols. These protocols mask the complexity of the hardware and the organization of exchanges. Services of information transfer over a network rely on communication protocols and software that are built according to a layered model and the end-to-end principle. These architectural principles offer an interesting and robust compromise between the need for reliability and that for performance. They are well adapted for low-to-average speeds and unreliable network infrastructures, both when transport needs are relatively homogeneous and when security constraints are rather low. In the context of high-speed networks and computing grid environments, the orders of magnitude and ratios of the constants in use are quite far from the hypotheses initially made for communication software protocols and architecture design. For example, the size of an Ethernet frame (between 64 and 1,500 bytes) – a parameter that indirectly conditions the maximum size of transfer units sent over an IP network – was defined to satisfy propagation constraints on a 200 m coaxial cable and a throughput of 10 Mbit/s. Today optical links are used and throughputs can be greater than 10 Gbit/s. At the time when the Internet Protocol (IP) was being designed, access rates were in the order of 64 kbit/s in wide-area networks. Today, optical fibers are deployed with access rates from 100 Mbit/s to 1 Gbit/s. There are links of over 100 Gbit/s in network cores.

In the Internet, since the workload is not controlled by the network itself, it is traditionally the transport layer – the first end-to-end layer – that carries out the adaptation to fluctuations in performance linked to load changes. The complexity of the transport layer depends on the quality of service offered by the underlying network in terms of strict delay or loss-ratio service guarantees. In the IP model, which offers a best-effort network service, two main transport protocols are classically used:

– a rudimentary protocol, the *User Datagram Protocol* or UDP, which only carries out stream multiplexing; and

– a very sophisticated reliable protocol, *Transmission Control Protocol* or TCP, which carries out the adaptation to packet losses as well as congestion control by send-rate control. TCP was designed for a network layer with no guaranteed quality of service (IP), for local-area networks and low-speed wide-area networks, and for a limited number of application classes.

The transport protocols are not really well adapted to very-high-speed infrastructures. Let us take the example of a simple TCP connection over a link between Lyon (France) and Montreal (Canada), with a round trip delay in the order of 100 ms and a 10 Gbit end-to-end throughput. Due to the design of the TCP congestion-avoidance algorithm, if one single packet is lost, it will take one hour and 40 minutes to repair and regain maximum speed. The TCP protocol is designed to react dynamically (i.e. in an interval of a few milliseconds) to congestion phenomena. It is not very reactive, however, in such conditions!

Over the past 10 years, a certain number of alternatives to TCP have been put forward and introduced in modern exploitation systems.

The protocol aspect is not the sole parameter to take into consideration for evaluating and improving end-to-end performance. Actually, in the very core of the communication nodes used, delays due to different data movement and control operations within a machine are significant compared to the delays encountered on the network itself (cables and routers). The heterogeneity of performance needs must also be taken into consideration.

The protocols used in the context of distributed computing have gradually became increasingly diverse because of the heterogeneity of the underlying physical technologies and applications needs. When the end-user of a cluster or a grid struggles to obtain the performance, however, he or she could expect delays with regard to the theoretical performance of the hardware used. He or she often has difficulties understanding where the problems with performance come from.

For this reason, this book invites the reader to concentrate more specifically on the core of distributed multi-machine architectures: the interconnection network and its communication protocols. The objective is to present, synthesize and articulate the different network technologies used by current and future distributed computing infrastructures. As these technologies are very heterogeneous in their physical characteristics and software, our aim is to propose the correct level of abstraction to help the reader structure and understand the main problems. It distinguishes the guidelines that, on the one hand, have oriented the technological evolution at the hardware and software levels, and on the other hand can guide programmers and users of distributed computing applications to adopt a programming model and an infrastructure adapted to their specific needs.

This book therefore has two objectives:

– to enable the reader who is familiar with communication networks to better understand the stakes and challenges that the new distributed computing revolution poses to networks and to their communication software;

– to enable the reader who is familiar with distributed computing to better understand the limits of current hardware and software tools, and how he or she can best adapt his or her application to the computing and communication infrastructure that is at his or her disposal to obtain the best possible performance.

To achieve these two objectives, we alternately move from one point of view to the other, introducing the core principles of distributed computing and networks and progressively detailing the most innovative approaches in these two fields.

In Chapter 1, we identify the needs, motivations and forces pushing the computer sector, over the years, towards distributed computing and the massive use of computing networks. We go into the details of the different network computing technologies that have evolved and show the technological and conceptual differences between them.

In Chapter 2 we classify distributed computing applications and analyze the communication specificities and constraints of each one of these classes of applications. In particular, we introduce the Message-Passing Interface communication library, or MPI, which is frequently used by distributed parallel application programmers.

In Chapter 3 we review the core principles of traditional communication networks and their protocols. We make an inventory of their limits compared to distributed computing constraints, which are introduced in the previous chapter. We then analyze the path of communications in a TCP/IP context.

The next two chapters are devoted to a detailed analysis of two major challenges that distributed computing poses to the network: latency and throughput. Two types of characteristic applications serve to illustrate their aim:

  – delay-sensitive parallel computing applications; and

  – communication-intensive, throughput-sensitive applications

In these chapters, we also discuss the direct interaction between the hardware level and the software level – a characteristic element of distributed computing.

Chapter 4 studies how the challenge of latency was overcome in computer cluster infrastructures to address the needs of applications that are very sensitive to information-routing delay between computing units.

Chapter 5 focuses on the needs of applications transferring significant masses of data in order to take them from their acquisition point to the computing centers where they are processed as well as to move them between storage spaces to conserve them and make them available to large and very scattered communities. We therefore study how the TCP protocol reacts in high bandwidth-delay product environments and detail the different approaches put forward to enable high-speed transport of information over very long distances.

Chapter 6 deals with performance measurement and prediction. It enables the reader, coming from the field of distributed computing, to understand the contributions of network performance measurement, prediction infrastructures and tools.

Chapter 7 shows how new optical switching technologies make it possible to provide a protected access to a communication capability adapted to the needs of each application.

Chapter 8 presents new dynamic bandwidth-management services, such as those currently proposed in the Open Grid Forum that suggest solutions for applications with sporadic needs relating to speeds that are not very high.

Chapter 9 introduces the issue of security and its principles in computing networks. This chapter presents the main solutions currently deployed as well as a few keys capable of increasing user confidence in distributed computing infrastructures.

Chapter 10 proposes a few protocol- and system-parameterization examples and exercises for obtaining high performance in a very-high-speed network with tools currently available in the Linux system.

To conclude, we summarize the different network technologies and protocols used in network computing, and provide a few perspectives for future networks that will integrate, among other things, our future worldwide computing power reserve.

Chapter 1

From Multiprocessor Computers to the Clouds

1.1. The explosion of demand for computing power

The demand for computing power continues to grow because of the technological advances in methods of digital acquisition and processing, the subsequent explosion of volumes of data, and the expansion of connectivity and information exchange. This ever-increasing demand varies depending on the scientific, industrial and domestic sectors considered.

Scientific applications have always needed increasing computing resources. Nevertheless, a new fact has appeared in the past few years: today's science relies on a very complex interdependence between disciplines, technologies and equipment.

In many disciplines the scientist can no longer work alone at his or her table or with his or her blank sheet of paper. He or she must rely on other specialists to provide him or her with the complementary and indispensable technical and methodological tools for his or her own research. This is what is called the development of multidisciplinarity.

For example, life science researchers today have to analyze enormous quantities of experimental data that can only be processed by multidisciplinary teams of experts carrying out complex studies and experiments and requiring extensive calculations. The organization of communities and the intensification of exchanges between researchers that has occurred over the past few years has increased the need to mutualize data and collaborate directly.

Thus these teams, gathering diverse and complementary expertise, demand cooperative work environments that enable them to analyze and visualize large groups of biological data, discuss the results and address questions of biological data in an interactive manner.

These environments must combine advanced visualization resources, broadband connectivity and access to important reserves of computing resources. With such environments, biologists hope, for example, to be able to analyze cell images at very high resolution. Current devices only enable portions of cells to be visualized, and this at a low level of resolution. It is also impossible to obtain contextual information such as the location in the cell, the type of cell or the metabolic state.

Another example is that of research on climate change. One of the main objectives is to calculate an adequate estimate of statistics of the variability of climate and thus anticipate the increase in greenhouse gas concentration. The study areas are very varied, going from ocean circulation stability to changes in atmospheric circulation on a continent. It also includes statistics on extreme events. It is a fundamental domain that requires the combination of a lot of data originating from sources that are very heterogeneous and by nature geographically remote. It involves the coupling of diverse mathematical models and crossing the varied and complementary points of view of experts.

As for industrial applications, the expansion and use of digital simulation increases the need for computing power. Digital simulation is a tool that enables the simulation of real and complex physical phenomena (resistance of a material, wearing away of a mechanism under different types of operating conditions, etc.) using a computer program. The engineer can therefore study the operation and properties of the system modeled and predict its evolution. Scientific digital simulations rely on the implementation of mathematical models that are often based on the finite elements technique and the visualization of computing results by computer-generated images. All of these calculations require great processing power.

In addition to this, the efficiency of computer infrastructure is a crucial factor in business. The cost of maintenance, but also, increasingly the cost of energy, can become prohibitive. Moreover, the need to access immense computing power can be sporadic. A business does not need massive resources to be continuously available. Only a few hours or a few nights per week can suffice: externalization and virtualization of computer resources has become increasingly interesting in this sector.

The domestic sector is also progressively requiring increased computing, storage and communication power. The Internet is now found in most homes in industrialized countries. The asymmetric digital subscriber line, otherwise known as ADSL is commonplace. In the near future Fiber To The Home (FTTH) will enable the diffusion of new domestic, social and recreational applications based, for example, on virtual-reality or increased-reality technologies, requiring tremendous computing capacities.

Computing resource needs are growing exponentially. Added to this, thanks to the globalization of trade, the geographical distribution of communicating entities has been amplified. To face these new challenges, three technologies have been developed in the past few years:

– computer clusters;

– computing grids; and

– computing and storage clouds.

In the following sections, we analyze the specificities of these different *network computing technologies* based on the most advanced communication methods and software.

1.2. Computer clusters

1.2.1. *The emergence of computer clusters*

The NOW [AND 95] and Beowulf [STE 95] projects in the 1990s launched the idea of aggregating hundreds of standard machines in order to form a high-power computing cluster. The initial interest lay in the highly beneficial *performance/price relationship* because aggregating standard materials was a lot cheaper than purchasing the specialized supercomputers that existed at the time. Despite this concept, achieving high computing power actually requires masking the structure of a cluster, particularly the time- and bandwidth-consuming communications between the different nodes. Many works were therefore carried out on the improvement of these communications in conjunction with the particular context of parallel applications that are executed on these clusters.

1.2.2. *Anatomy of a computer cluster*

Server clusters or computer farms designate the local collection of several independent computers (called nodes) that are globally run and destined to surpass the limitations of a single computer. They do this in order to:

– increase computing power and availability;

– facilitate load increase;

– enable load balancing;

– simplify the management of resources (central processing unit or CPU, memory, disks and network bandwidth).

Figure 1.1 highlights the hierarchical structure of a cluster organized around a network of interconnected equipment (switches). The

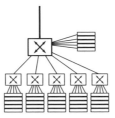

Figure 1.1. *Typical architecture of a computer cluster*

machines making up a *server cluster* are generally of the same type. They are stacked up in racks and connected to switches. Therefore systems can evolve based on need: nodes are added and connected on demand. This type of aggregate, much cheaper than a multiprocessor server, is frequently used for parallel computations. Optimized use of resources enables the distribution of data processing on the different nodes. Clients communicate with a cluster as if it were a single machine. Clusters are normally made up of three or four types of nodes:

– computing nodes (the most numerous – there are generally 16, 32, 64, 128 or 256 of them);

– storage nodes (fewer than about 10);

– front-end nodes (one or more);

– there may also be additional nodes dedicated to system surveillance and measurement.

Nodes can be linked to each other by several networks:

– the computing network, for exchanges between processes; and

– the administration and control network (loading of system images on nodes, follow-up, load measurement, etc.).

To ensure a large enough bandwidth during the computing phases, computing network switches generally have a large number of ports. Each machine, in theory, has the same bandwidth for communicating with other machines linked to the same equipment. This is called *full bandwidth bisection*. The computing network is characterized by a very broad bandwidth and above all has a very low latency. This network is a *high performance* network and is often based on a specific communication topology and technology (see Chapter 2). The speeds of computing networks can reach 10 Gbit/s between each machine, and latency can be as low as a few nanoseconds. The control network is a classic Ethernet local area network with a speed of 100 Mbit/s or 1 Gbit/s. The parallel programs executed on clusters often use the Message Passing Interface communication library, enabling messages to be exchanged between the different processors distributed on the nodes. Computing clusters are used for high performance computing in digital imagery, especially for computer-generated images computed in render farms.

Should a server fail, the administration software of the cluster is capable of transferring the tasks executed on the faulty server to the other servers in the cluster. This technology is used in information system management to increase the availability of systems. Disk farms shared and linked by a storage area network are an example of this technology.

1.3. Computing grids

The term "grid" was introduced at the end of the 1990s by Ian Foster and Carl Kesselman [FOS 04] and goes back to the idea of aggregating and sharing the distributed computing power inherent in the concept of metacomputing which has been studied since the 1980s. *The principal specificity of grids is to enable the simple and transparent use of computing resources as well data spread out across the world without worrying about their location.*

Computing grids are distributed systems that combine heterogeneous and high-performance resources connected by a wide-area network (WAN). The underlying vision of the grid concept is to offer access to a quasi-unlimited capacity of information-processing facilities – *computing power* – in a way that is as simple and ubiquitous as electric power access. Therefore, a simple connection enables us to get access to a *global and virtual computer*. According to this vision, computing power would be delivered by many computing resources, such as computing servers and data servers available to all through a universal network.

In a more formal and realistic way, grid computing is an evolution of distributed computing based on dynamic resource sharing between participants, organizations and businesses. It aims to mutualize resources to execute intensive computing applications or to process large volumes of data.

Indeed, whereas the need for computing power is becoming increasingly important, it has become ever more sporadic. Computing power is only needed during certain hours of the day, certain periods of the year or in the face of certain exceptional events. Each organization or business, not being able to acquire oversized computing equipment for temporary use, decides to mutualize its computing resources with those of other organizations. Mutualization on an international scale offers the advantage of benefiting from time differences and re-using the resources of others during the day where it is nighttime where they are. The grid therefore appeared as a new approach promising to provide a large number of scientific domains, and more recently industrial communities, with the computing power they need.

Time-sharing of resources offers an economical and flexible solution to access the power required. From the user's point of view, theoretically the origin of the resources used is totally abstract and transparent. The user, in the end, should not worry about anything: neither the power necessary for his or her applications, nor the type of machines used. He or she should worry even less about the physical location of the machines being used. Ideally, it is the grid platform management and supervision software that runs all these aspects.

The concept of the grid is therefore particularly powerful because it offers many perspectives to the computer science domain. Indeed, it enables providers of computing facilities to:

– make the resource available at the time it is necessary;

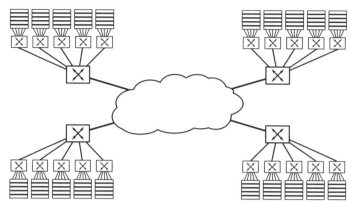

Figure 1.2. *Systematic architecture of a computing grid: interconnection of clusters across a wide-area network*

– make the resource consumable on an on-demand basis, and this in a simple and transparent way;

– make it possible to use and share the capacity of unused resources;

– limit the cost of the computer resource to the part that is really consumed.

Furthermore, for the user, the reasons that justify the development and deployment of applications on computing grids are mainly:

– the increase in and sporadic nature of computing power demand;

– the need for dynamic resolution of increasingly complex problems;

– the need for large-scale sharing of information or rare and costly equipment.

The grid concept has been studied intensely by researchers since the end of the 1990s. The concept and its definition have not stopped evolving over time. The technologies and standards that materialize from the use of grids follow their maturing process. From the time it appeared, the grid concept – which is much more ambitious than that of the cluster – has raised very strong interest in the scientific community as well as the general public. It has been seen as the new level of computing technology in general. The main reason is that the term "grid computing" refers to an analogy with the electricity distribution network, which is called the power grid.

The grid was first defined as a material and software infrastructure giving reliable and universal access to very high-performance computing and storage resources. This definition was revised in the 2000s. The notion of service was substituted for the concept of resource. The Open Grid Services Architecture or OGSA, for example, merges the concepts of the grid and web services. The coordination of shared resources, dynamic problem-solving and concurrent use by different communities (or virtual organizations) became the leading topics. Today the resources considered are not only distributed computers and shared storage facilities, but also network elements, mobile terminals, sensor networks, large data-acquisition instruments, very high-definition viewing devices as well as databases and application codes. The term "grid" is therefore often associated with a large variety of different meanings and notions.

Two large grid system families have been developed:
– high-performance grids; and
– peer-to-peer grids.

1.3.1. *High-performance computing grids*

The objective of a high-performance grid is to provide very large computing power by a high-powered computer or computer cluster aggregation. These grids are generally made up of resources from virtual organizations that decide to mutualize their resources. They are generally designed for processing massive amounts of data from large scientific communities. In principle, the resources contribute 100% of their time to the global infrastructure. In general, an adequately dimensioned optical network, which is often dedicated to the role, interconnects the different participating sites. The resources of these systems are relatively static.

1.3.2. *Peer-to-peer computing grids*

The objective of a "peer-to-peer" or P2P grid is to enable large computations to be solved by benefiting from the unused computing capacity of participating nodes. These worker nodes are usually isolated and made available by dispersed users. The equipment is voluntarily enrolled by its owner, who permits it to be used by a collective P2P computing application when idling. In these grids, resources are therefore volatile and the performance of communications is very hard to predict.

The term *grid* remains associated with the scientific domain. In theory, grid computing tends to go beyond the services offered by the traditional Internet, by making computing and communications converge. In practice, however, this concept is very difficult to implement and use. The deployment and use of current grids requires significant expertise as well as a non-negligible investment on the user's part. Therefore, outside a few limited applications such as SETI@home, the grid has failed to gain popularity with the general public and small-to medium-sized businesses.

The ideal of a grid that exploits all unused resources from each computer has remained the preserve of a minority of businesses. What is possible for large businesses or research centers, however, could also be achieved by the general public, be it at an individual or a local community level. The latter actually have large number of pieces of computer equipment and in the near future will need computer power 10 times as great in order to be able to use the new virtual reality and 3D simulation tools. Many communities could organize their computer equipment into grids, without any price increase, in order to have computing power at their disposal corresponding to their future needs. This would be done by making some of the communities' servers available to other communities.

As a first step, businesses or communities could create a grid that places a few dozen specialized and standardized servers in a network. These servers would be linked to each other by a high-speed link and carry out computations for researchers working for a public organization or a large business. For example, many research and development centers could mutualize all their computers to carry out jobs that are particularly demanding in computing power.

It is this idea that was successfully developed and implemented in the experimental Grid5000, which is the daily work tool for several hundreds of computer science researchers and students in France [BOL 06a, CAP 05].

Grid5000 is an experimental grid platform, the purpose of which is to study algorithms and protocols for intensive distributed computing and P2P applications. This instrument, the only one of its kind in the world because of its technical specificities, gathers more than 5,000 computing cores. These are divided into nine clusters located in different regions of France and interconnected by a dedicated optical network, provided by the French National Telecommunications Network for Technology, Teaching and Research (RENATER). Grid5000 has a very powerful mechanism for automatic reconfiguration of all the processors. Researchers can therefore deploy, install, run and execute their operating system images – including their own stack of network protocols – in order to communicate on the private network. This capability for reconfiguration has led users of Grid5000 to adopt the following workflow:

(1) reserve a partition of Grid5000 (group of machines);

(2) deploy a software image on each of the reserved nodes;

(3) reboot all the machines of the partition with this new software image;

(4) run the experiment;

(5) collect results;

(6) release the machines in an automated operation that re-initializes the memory and temporary files.

Grid5000 enables the reproduction of experimental conditions: network links are dedicated, users can reserve exactly the same set of resources during successive experiments, install and activate their own experimental conditions and measurement software. For a time limited to the reservation period, the user has total control over the set of reserved resources. The Grid5000 infrastructure gradually extends internationally and integrates remote sites via virtual private links, as indicated in Figure 3.1.

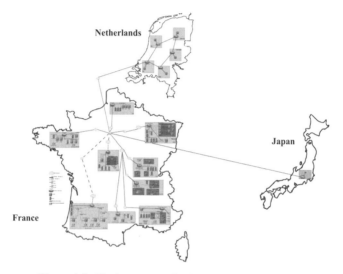

Figure 1.3. *The international infrastructure of Grid5000*

1.4. Computing in a cloud

Having emerged in 2007, the concept of cloud computing pushes the idea of transparency and virtualization of resources even further than grid computing does. Cloud computing is a concept that refers to the use of processing and storage capacities of servers distributed throughout the world and linked by a network, such as the Internet.

The basic principle is similar to the initial vision of grid computing, but it is essentially the implementation of cloud computing that differentiates it. Indeed, unlike the grid, the communities of users or individual users do not own the computer servers making up the infrastructure. They access external resources online without having to manage the underlying hardware, which is complex to install, configure and keep up-to-date, and is subject to failures. Whereas in the grid the economic model is based on the reciprocity of supply and maintenance of resources, in cloud computing the user pays per use (typically, a few dollars to rent a remote processor for a few hours). The applications and data are not deployed on the user's local computer, but – metaphorically speaking – in a cloud composed of a huge number of interconnected remote servers. The computation results are retransmitted to the client or sent over other specified sites. Access to the service is through a readily available standard application, usually a web browser. In the grid the user invokes a job execution service by using a specific description language (Job Description Language or JDL). To use the computing power in the cloud, on the other hand, an access service to virtual resources is invoked. The service given is of a lower abstraction level and is therefore easier to account and bill than in a grid.

The cloud therefore represents an abstract infrastructure supplying resources and their associated services via the Internet. It is primarily aimed at customers that were not able to access the grid: private individuals and small- and medium-sized businesses. Every type of management, communication, business and/or leisure application is capable of using the resource services offered by cloud computing technology because it is available from any computer connected to the Internet.

Various types of clouds are available:

– a storage cloud offers storage services (services at the block or file level);

– a data cloud provides data-management services (based on records, columns or objects); and

– a computing cloud exposes data-processing services.

These clouds are often organized into layers and present a stack of cloud services that act as a computing platform for developing distributed applications. By providing an invisible and extendable infrastructure service, the infrastructure as a service (IaaS) paradigm perfectly completes the software as a service (SaaS) concept, which deals with the management of software licenses that are predeployed and made available to users. The majority of cloud computing infrastructures are made up of reliable services provided by data-processing centers that rely on computing- and storage-virtualization technologies.

Cloud computing relies on the Internet's availability and connectivity. Nevertheless, excellent bandwidth will quickly be mandatory to the fluidity of such a system. Finely-tuned, high-speed Internet connections are seen as a major factor of the deployment of cloud computing, enabling optimization of the response time of an infrastructure currently designed in a centralized way.

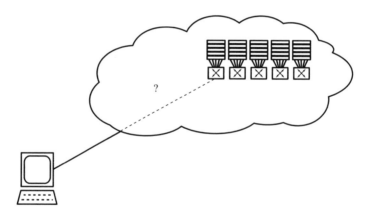

Figure 1.4. *Systematic architecture of a computing cloud*

Cloud computing has created a true revolution in the computing world. Led by software and Internet service companies, such as Amazon and Google, as well as by suppliers of computer equipment, such as IBM or SUN, this new wave has completely overshadowed the grid world, from which it took its initial vision. It has introduced it on a large scale to the general public and small businesses. The most significant examples of cloud computing services are:

– EC2 infrastructures (Elastic Compute Cloud);

– S3 storage cloud;

– Amazon's SimpleDB data cloud;

– Google File System (GFS);

– Google BigTable;

– Google MapReduce; and

– the open-source system Hadoop.

Google GFS is, for example, capable of running petabytes of data. Three levels of cloud services are distinguished:

– IaaS;

– platform as a service (PaaS); and

– SaaS.

Below we concentrate more on the aspect of IaaS, which deals with the supply of digital resources over the Internet.

Returning to the idea of the grid and the metaphor of the electric power distribution system, the concept of cloud computing above all introduces an economic model, a very simple security model and architecture. Computing and information-storage power is offered for consumption by specialized companies. The customer only communicates with a single supplying entity that offers a unique portal and, quite often, relies on a centralized infrastructure. For this reason, businesses no longer need to acquire and maintain their own servers but can invest in renting this resource from a service supplier who guarantees computing and storage power on demand. Billing is based on the computing power and duration actually consumed.

By being less complex than the grid, cloud computing can easily be used by small – and medium – sized businesses and the general public. Data clouds provide important advantages compared to other technologies in the management and analysis of data. For the majority of applications, databases make up the preferred infrastructure for managing data sets. As the size of these data sets increases and reaches several hundred terabytes, more specialized solutions such as storage services will become more competitive than classic databases.

1.5. Conclusion

In the previous sections, we have seen that the concepts of computing clusters, grids and clouds have followed each other by subtly competing with one another. Clusters aggregate individual computers that are interconnected by a local network in order to supply a greater computing power at low cost. Grids link up heterogeneous resources, often computer clusters, via a WAN to mutualize and spread out resources. The cloud, through a paid and secured service, enables the remote and transparent use of clusters or grids composed of rare and/or powerful resources whether interconnected with each other or not. Furthermore, for intensive computing infrastructures there is a return in interest with regards to massive parallelism using multicore approaches and petascale systems. For the sake of coherence and conciseness, in this book we do not develop these new approaches as, from the point of view of the network, they pose problems similar to those encountered in high-performance networks for computer clusters studied, which is discussed in Chapter 4.

Developed about 10 years ago and having stimulated a large amount of research and experiments, grid platforms fill the gap between science and technology and provide the infrastructure and resources required by science today. It is believed that, in the near future, these technologies will be combined with other innovations and will be fully integrated in the Internet to supply the computing, storage and cooperation power required by our modern companies. This will be achieved in an efficient, economic and ecological way. Cloud computing is the new wave that overshadows this formidable mutation.

In Chapter 2 we detail the different classes of applications that run on these computing infrastructures. These very diverse applications can have different sensitivities to the performance of communications. We analyze, in particular, the place and constraints of the network within these infrastructures. We present the challenges posed to network technologies to enable computing networks to reach their full potential and for their users to benefit to the greatest degree from them.

	Appearance	Unit component	Type of network	Use
Supercomputer	1980s	processor	internal bus	intensive parallel
Cluster	1990	standard PC	high performance	intensive parallel
Grid	1999	PC or PC cluster	high speed	intensive distributed
Multicores	2005	processor	high performance	intensive parallel
Cloud	2007	PC, cluster, grid	Internet	remote computing
Petascale machines	2010	multicore blades	high performance	intensive parallel

Table 1.1. *Classification of distributed and parallel computing infrastructures*

Chapter 2

Utilization of Network Computing Technologies

In less than 20 years, parallel and distributed computing infrastructures have experienced three profound revolutions: clusters, grids and clouds. Each of these technologies is more or less adapted to certain types of use. In this chapter we present the anatomy of distributed computing applications and then give a classification of these applications. The objective is to highlight factors that should guide the user when choosing one or other type of infrastructure and the network or protocol designer when choosing this or that technical approach.

2.1. Anatomy of a distributed computing application

Digital simulation and complex analyses of large quantities of data are characteristic examples of applications that can benefit from a high-performance distributed computing environment. Digitally simulating a physical system (a car, plane, nuclear power plant, etc.) consists of solving equations that model the system's behavior in space. Typically, the problem is broken down into a spatial mesh divided into several parts. As an example, the digital model of the plane or that of the space in which it will evolve can be considered as being divided into several pieces. Next, piece by piece, the interactions between these different systems are calculated. Then, to simulate the system's behavior in time, these equation sets are resolved iteratively.

In another family of applications – called stochastic or optimization applications – the problem is split up into independent parts, or several instances of the same problem are calculated independently in parallel.

Therefore, these applications often use parallel-computing techniques to accelerate the resolution of a problem that can be very large in size and can sometimes require several days of computing on a simple processor.

When the job is distributed, each part or instance of the problem is calculated by a different computer. When the distributed tasks work in parallel, they sometimes have data or intermediate results to exchange.

For example, in Figure 2.1, the program is broken down into six tasks (P1 to P6), also sometimes called processes or jobs. P1, P2 and P3 are executed in parallel and are synchronized at the level of task P4. P4 then distributes the job so that P5 and P6 can be executed in parallel. The input data of this program are File 1 and File 2. The result is returned at the end of the program in File 3.

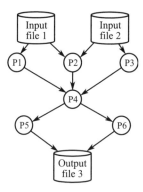

Figure 2.1. *Task sequence of a complex application*

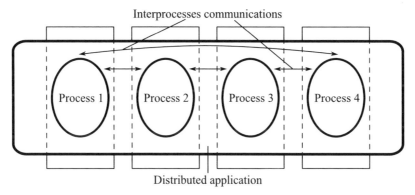

Figure 2.2. *Diagram of the distribution of a multiprocess application*

Figure 2.2 shows how the different tasks of the application above can be distributed (or mapped) over desktop computers.

2.1.1. *Parallelization and distribution of an algorithm*

The nature and intensity of communications between tasks greatly influence computing time and therefore the choice of distributed infrastructure. Exchanges between blocks are very quick on a parallel machine because they are done directly through shared memory. In a cluster, messages pass through the interconnection network. If the application is run on a computing grid where the network latency is greater than a millisecond, coupling between tasks or computing blocks will be more relaxed than when it is run on a cluster or a parallel computer. Applications are often classified according to how often their subtasks need to synchronize or communicate with each other. An application exhibits fine-grained parallelism if its subtasks must communicate many times per second; it exhibits coarse-grained parallelism if they do not communicate many times per second, and it is embarrassingly parallel if they rarely or never have to communicate. Embarrassingly parallel applications are considered the easiest to parallelize.

2.1.1.1. *Embarrassingly parallel applications*

In some applications, data domains can be completely divided in advance and the data distributed upon initialization. These applications are said to be *embarrassingly parallel*. The distribution of initial data on different computers corresponds to the preprocessing phase (*stage-in*). In general, a process, called the *master* process, is in charge of data distribution and activation of processes called *workers*. Each process works on its own data on an independent computer. In the end, the results are collected to be stored or displayed. This is the *post-processing* phase (*stage-out*).

The programming model "MapReduce" for processing masses of data on a large number of computers is a very popular, particularly in the case of this type of embarrassingly parallel application. Processing can be carried out on data stored in a file system (unstructured) or in a database (structured). This framework corresponds to a large number of data-mining applications, e.g. searches for web pages containing a key word (search engine).

In the *Map* stage, a master node takes the mass of input data and cuts it up finely into sub-problems, which it distributes to *worker* nodes. A worker node can in turn re-do some cutting, which leads to a multilevel tree structure. In the *Reduce* stage, the master node takes the answers for all of the sub-problems and combines them in such a way as to get the answer to the problems submitted. The advantage of MapReduce is that it enables all the operations to be processed in a distributed and theoretically parallel way. Today MapReduce can be used on a large-sized server cluster to sort a petabyte of data in only a few hours. Parallelism also offers the possibility of supporting server or storage breakdowns during the operation: if a mapper or a reducer fails, the job can be transferred to another processor.

The distribution, *Map* and the *Reduce* functions of MapReduce are defined in relation to data structured in (key, value) pairs. *Map* takes one pair of data with a type in the data domain and returns a list of pairs in a different domain:

$$\mathrm{Map}(k1, v1) \longrightarrow \mathrm{list}(k2, v2).$$

2.1.1.1.1. The *Map* function

The *Map* function is applied in parallel to each element in the input dataset. This produces a list of $(k2, v2)$ pairs for each call. After that, MapReduce collects all the pairs with the same key from all the lists and groups them together, thus creating a group for each of the different keys generated. The *Reduce* function is then applied in parallel to each group which, in turn, produces a collection of values in the same domain:

$$\mathrm{Reduce}\left(k2, \mathrm{list}(v2)\right) \longrightarrow \mathrm{list}(v3)$$

2.1.1.1.2. The *Reduce* call

Each *Reduce* call generally produces either a value, $v3$, or an empty return. The returns of all calls are collected in the desired results list. Thus, the MapReduce framework transforms a list of (key, value) pairs into a list of values. In MapReduce, data exchanges are produced at the end of each processing step. The tasks are completely independent.

2.1.1.2. *Fine-grained parallelism*

When in the parallelization phase of an application, data split-up cannot be completely clear and a non-empty intersection remains between the subdomains. Intermediate data must be communicated from one computer to the other. These exchanges take place during the processing phase, at each iteration step for example. This is called inter-process communication (IPC). Parallel applications that communicate during computing phases are said to exhibit *fine-grained parallelism*.

Some applications can show a hybrid structure or be even more complex. For example, the family of physical simulation applications – which includes applications for structural mechanics, fluid dynamics, molecular dynamics, electromagnetics, chemistry, materials science, seismology, reservoirs, meteorology, virtual reality, etc. – are often heterogeneous and consume large volumes of data. They often have distributed and asynchronous control and are constructed in layers and by composition. In these applications, a large number of proprietary components are found. Each component implements a part or a stage of the simulation that can be implemented in parallel with, for example, the Message Passing Interface or MPI library, *threads* or even vector processing.

2.1.2. *Modeling parallel applications*

Parallel applications are generally modeled in the form of graphs representing the logical progression of the processing. Some complex applications are expressed using *workflows*; others are carried out in *batch* sequential processing via *batch queues* on computers with varied architecture. Workflows used for describing complex applications are graphs indicating the modules to execute and the existing relations or data dependencies between the modules. Figure 2.3 represents a workflow of an application for processing medical images. To run such applications on computing grids, specific tools capable of analyzing and executing a workflow description file were developed [GLA 08]. Figure 2.4 represents a distribution of the tasks of this medical application. For fine-grained applications, the dependences between elementary tasks are generally represented by a graph of tasks or directed acyclic graph (DAG).

2.1.3. *Example of a grid application*

One of the great challenges of modern physics is to answer the fundamental question: why do particles have a mass? For this, we must explore the physical world in a state similar to that at the time of the Big Bang. Such a study requires very costly machines (similar to large microscopes) and work programs that can last more than 20 years. This is the reason why the community of high-energy physicians became equipped with a 17 km ring constructed at the European Organization

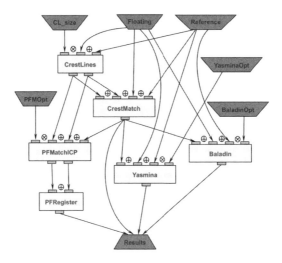

Figure 2.3. *Workflow of a medical-imagery application*

for Nuclear Research or CERN in Switzerland. It forms a global instrument shared by 2,000 physicians belonging to 150 universities distributed in 34 countries and is called the *Large Hadron Collider* or LHC.

The energy level required by these experiments is seven times greater than that required by traditional instruments used by physicians and the rate of data generated is 40 times greater. In this ring, 150 million sensors acquire petabytes of data per second. These raw data are filtered and coded and generate 15 petabytes of data each year. These data require immense storage space and about 100,000 processors for processing them. These enormous data collections are shared by a very large number of users, each with unforeseeable data-access patterns.

Therefore, instead of creating a gigantic and extremely difficult to maintain computing center, the community preferred to equip the LHC with a worldwide computing grid. The *Large Collider Grid* or LCG is the operating infrastructure for data generated by the CERN's LHC. The

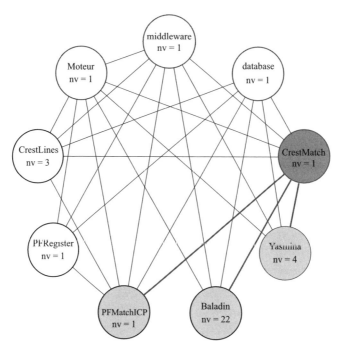

Figure 2.4. *Task graph of the medical application in Figure 2.3*

model adopted in order to store and process data is highly hierarchical, as shown in Figure 2.5.

CERN is at the top of this hierarchical data tree (level-0 tier). About 10 big computing centers (level-1 tiers) are distributed throughout the continents. These centers replicate, store and process all the data. Below this, there are level-2 and level-3 tiers that are available to researchers in their respective regions. In this grid, the wide-area network (WAN) plays a central role. It is a private optical network that links CERN's site with the first-level (tier 1) sites in a star topology and then the second-level (tier 2) sites in series; see Figure 2.5. This network is based on virtual private network services at 1 or 10 Gbit/s (see Chapter 6) supplied by national and international research networks, for example GEANT in Europe.

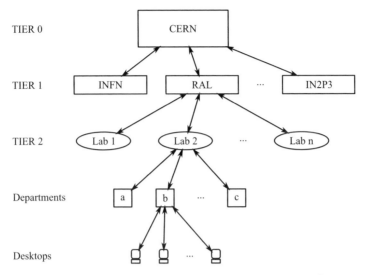

Figure 2.5. *Hierarchical architecture of the LCG data grid*

2.1.4. *General classification of distributed applications*

Intensive distributed computing applications are classified according to two important characteristics: computing intensity and data intensity. Computing intensity is defined as being the computing quantity per unit of data transferred between processes or read from a storage space. Data intensity is the opposite of computing intensity, i.e. the quantity of data processed per computing unit.

The useful metrics for these two types of applications are run time and processing speed. *Run time* (*turnaround* or *completion time*) is the duration that separates a task being started and the results being obtained. It is the performance metric in which the user of a computing infrastructure is most interested. *Throughput* is the volume of entries possible without affecting the run time of individual applications. It is this usage metric that the system's owner tries to optimize.

There are several classifications of computing applications [FOS 04, VIC 07]. Analysis of underlying algorithms and scenarios for the use of grid applications has brought five main application classes to the fore that are differentiated by their computing intensity in terms of memory space required, data locality and inter-task communication needs. Thus, in this book we distinguish the following five classes, ordered according to the severity of their resource constraints:

– widely distributed computing;

– loosely coupled computing;

– pipeline computing;

– highly synchronized computing;

– interactive and collaborative computing.

2.1.4.1. *Widely distributed computing*

The applications of this class perform research or modifications, or they unify distributed databases, for example. Computing, memory and data needs are low. The main problem to solve involves effectively enabling remote access to co-localized data and processing resources, with different updating rights and operations. They are applications that are often data-related but not necessarily data-intensive. Computing on demand (cloud computing), which requires access to remote resources to execute a computation, also fall into this category.

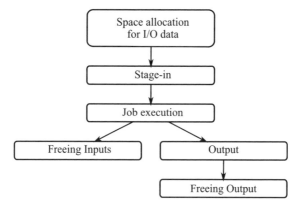

Figure 2.6. *Principles of stage-in and stage-out phases in a distributed application*

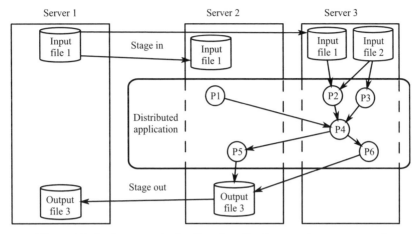

Figure 2.7. *Deployment of a distributed application over three servers and stage-in and stage-out phases*

2.1.4.2. *Loosely coupled computing*

The applications in this category are composed of *bags-of-tasks* with low memory needs, few data per task and little inter-task communication. When there are a very large number of such tasks showing low coupling, it is called high-throughput computing. Communications between the computer, the source(s) and/or data sink(s) are often intense in the pre-processing (stage-in) or post-processing (stage-out) phases. Figure 2.6 explains the logical sequence of stage-in and stage-out phases with the rest of the computation. Figure 2.7 shows the communications necessary for routing input data during the stage-in phase to computing resources. Data sources can be digital libraries, sensor networks, acquisition instruments, distributed databases and warehouses. Typical examples of this group include:

– data-grid applications, such as the CERN's LCG grid;

– biocomputing;

– finance; and

– networks for fast reaction to natural disasters.

Thus, they are computing-intensive but can be conveniently executed on clusters that are highly distributed and connected by low-bandwidth, high-latency networks. On the other hand, interconnections between data warehouses and computers must enable high-speed transfers during the pre- and post-processing phases.

2.1.4.3. *Pipeline computing*

Pipeline computing applications absorb continuous (streamed) or real-time data. The underlying algorithms are generally memory-consuming and data-intensive. They have an embarrassingly parallel inter-task communication, whereas the tasks themselves are highly parallel. Their data-storage and memory needs are more important than in widely distributed computing, as are their communication needs during the processing phase. Typical examples in this class are real-time signal processing applications and applications related to the filtering/storage of data captured by satellites, sensors, microscopes, etc. By nature, problems are distributed: acquisition resources cannot be co-localized with computing resources or storage spaces.

2.1.4.4. *Highly synchronized computing*

Applications from this class have very frequent inter-task synchronizations. Such applications include, for example, applications of climate modeling, or physical or molecular phenomena based on explicit iterative methods (cellular automata).

These distributed parallel-computing applications are initially created to use tightly coupled platforms, such as the large parallel systems or large computer clusters. They are implemented by several iterative and competing threads that strongly interact during computing. This task parallelism enables greater computation, at a faster rate. Large volumes of data can be manipulated. Computing power and memory needs can be significant. They can therefore be simultaneously data- and computing-intensive and inherit the need for pipeline computing. They add an extra demand regarding network infrastructure because they require a significant amount of fine-grained communications.

Applications of this class require so-called high-performance computing (HPC) systems. They are the most difficult applications to distribute.

2.1.4.5. *Interactive and collaborative computing*

This class of application is characterized by the potential interaction of the user during computing. In collaborative applications, several users can intervene during processing or visualize the results. It is often necessary to implement an entire collaborative environment with audio and video facilities to facilitate interactions and decisions.

Collaborative use of the grid accelerates interaction between geographically-distributed users thanks to shared visual spaces. The application for interactive visualization of digital simulation results on a very large video wall ($5\,m \times 3\,m$) studied in the Carriocas project is a good example of this [AUD 09]. These applications have external sources of information (which can themselves be other grid applications), a remote display and information-processing pipelines that link the source to the display.

2.1.4.6. *Note*

This classification does not capture all the possible dimensions of distributed intensive-computing applications. Reality is often considerably more complex. Some real applications cover several classes. This classification, however, highlights reasonably strong locality and performance criteria (quality of service or QoS), directly influencing the choice of the type of infrastructure. Also, as we will see in the next chapter, it influences the characteristics expected from the interconnection network and its protocols. Typically, tightly coupled applications are very sensitive to latency and are most efficient when executed on a computing cluster with a high-performance network (see Chapter 3). High-speed applications are those that can best benefit from the computing grid; whereas individual, on-demand computing applications run efficiently on a computing cloud.

2.2. Programming models of distributed parallel applications

2.2.1. *Main models*

Communication programming models enable the application programmer to define the system mechanisms used by the different parallel and/or distributed computing tasks. Different programming models authorize different communication styles between application processes during the execution of an application. These models are distinguished by their level of abstraction and their ability to mask the exchanges and hardware details of the network.

The main paradigms are the following:

(1) basic socket programming;

(2) message-passing via a specialized library (e.g. MPI);

(3) shared memory;

(4) remote calling;

(5) remote access.

Many distributed applications communicate using the Socket interface, which traditionally uses the Transport Control Protocol (TCP) or User Datagram Protocol (UDP). Parallel applications generally rely on dedicated paradigms of the message-passing or shared-memory type in which communication details are concealed. In applications based on the client-server model, the remote method invocation (RMI, CORBA) or remote procedure call (RPC) is very wide spread. Programming multiprocess applications are complex, even if these models and the tools that come with them aim to limit the complexity. These different models were adapted with relative success and performance to the different infrastructures, whether homogeneous or heterogeneous.

The choice of programming model is left to the application programmer, who tends to favor the approach he or she knows best. There is therefore a very large diversity in the use of these paradigms and there is no clearly-established relationship between the model and type of application seen in the classification above, even if some models are theoretically better adapted than others to certain use cases.

2.2.2. *Constraints of fine-grained-parallelism applications*

Intensive scientific computing displays very specific and different needs from communications-based distributed systems, for example, on the client-server model. With the objective being the execution of computing as quickly as possible, this type of processing is distributed across different machines. The total quantity of data to process can currently reach the terabyte level. It therefore cannot be stored in each of the nodes but must be distributed. The greater the computing needs, the higher the number of machines necessary. Modern clusters often gather together several thousand machines. Finally, interdependence between different computing methods implies simultaneous execution, and comparatively periodic synchronizations and communications between the different processes in order to exchange intermediary results. The final aspect of a parallel application therefore consists of running a similar program in each processor of each node that works on a specific subset of data and regularly exchanges information.

This model is very different from the general distributed-systems model, where a variable number of machines can run rather random applications and communicate rather haphazardly. Parallel applications have better-mastered communication diagrams (as they are defined according to the algorithm implemented by the application) but also have significant synchronization and communication requirements, and this with a potentially vast number of machines. Thus, in a cluster, geographically-close machines (gathered in a single room) will be preferred to very distant machines. This proximity drastically modifies retransmission and congestion-control needs.

Adapted protocols have proven to be necessary. Parallel-computing applications are therefore not satisfied with the additional costs imposed by classic communication protocols, which are due to different execution conditions (distance, reliability, etc.). Besides, the memory copies imposed by the operating system's protocol layers limit communication speed and consume processor time that the application could have at its disposal. The additional latency costs imposed by the crossing of these software layers and the notification of network events can noticeably slow down the applications. The specific needs of parallel-application communications have therefore favored the emergence of a dedicated programming interface – the MPI, the details of which we will go into in the next section. In addition to this, many reflections have been carried out on network hardware and the software stack exploiting it, the details of which we will go into in Chapter 3.

2.2.3. The MPI communication library

In order to be better adapted to the very specific context and needs of scientific parallel-computing applications, a dedicated programming interface was put forward challenging the standard Socket interface. The first version was introduced in 1994 by the MPI Forum [FOR 94]. MPI is neither a language nor a layout. It is a standard designed for parallelizing scientific computing applications on parallel machines and clusters. It is a set of C and Fortran functions implemented by many libraries, the most famous of which are MPICH and OpenMPI.

MPI's programming paradigm is the *passage of messages*. In contrast to data streams in the synchronous connections of the Socket model, each message-sending operation corresponds exactly to a message reception, whatever the size may be. For example, if an application wants to send four bytes then six, it will be able to receive the 10 bytes in one go with the Socket interface. On the other hand, in MPI it will be necessary to post two reception requests: one for each one sent. The notion of "request" is at the heart of the programming model because all communication operations are based on it. It is therefore a matter of posting *point-to-point* communication requests (sending or receiving) or *collective* operations. The operations supported are in fact strongly linked to the needs of parallel applications, particularly those linear algebra ones where sets of matrix blocks must frequently be exchanged. For example an *all-to-all* communication enables data exchange between all processes, as represented in Figure 2.8, whereas a *Reduce* communication will accumulate data from all processes on one specific process in order to synthesize its contributions at the end of computing.

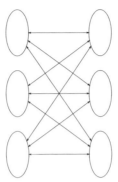

Figure 2.8. *MPI all-to-all communication*

Submitting these requests can be non-blocking and the application will then have to test the request terminations later. The non-blocking aspect is primordial because theoretically it enables computing to overlap communications, instead of waiting without doing anything until the request is terminated. The application can therefore benefit by using the available processing time to carry out useful jobs. Different tags can, in addition, be used in order to mark different types of independent communication, for example control and data messages. The operation associating an input message and a reception request available with the same tag is called matching.

More than the operations themselves, it is the entire communication model that is different. First of all, each process participating in the execution of a parallel application can be identified by a *rank* that enables communication with it, much like an IP address and a process identifier. Indeed, since parallel applications execute a set of identical processes simultaneously on a set of known machines, each process has knowledge of all the others and is therefore easily able to communicate with them, thanks to this rank.

Then, since parallel computing, e.g. matrix computing, often hands out different subsets of work to different subsets of processes, the notions of *communicator* and *groups* were defined. Each process has a rank in each communicator to which it belongs and it is thus, for example, possible to implement collective operations based solely on one subset of processes.

Finally, MPI enables the application to clearly expose the organization of data in memory in order to benefit from potential software or hardware optimizations. Datatypes, for example, allow a matrix column to be sent by specifying its characteristics, without giving the set of positions of the different memory segments. During reception, the application can use another datatype to receive data based on another memory organization, which, for example, enables the implementation of an on-the-fly matrix transposition.

The MPI interface initially seemed very complex but was finally imposed as the communication standard for parallel applications, for lack of better options. Industrialists attempted to impose other programming interfaces, Virtual Interface Architecture (VIA) in particular [SPE 99] and more recently Direct Access Portable Layer (DAPL) [COL 07], which offer non-blocking primitives in connected mode. This model was never imposed, however, mainly because the message-passing model put forward by MPI turned out to be more practical and efficient for receiving parallel computing applications [BRI 00].

The MPI norm has been regularly extended since its creation in 1993. It saw the addition of dynamic process management in MPI-2[1] and was generalized for input-output to storage with extension MPI-IO[2]. Ongoing discussions to define the third version of the norm aim, among other things, to add the support of non-blocking collective operations in

---

1. MPI-2: Extensions to the Message Passing Interface, http://www.mpi-forum.org/docs/mpi-20-html/mpi2-report.html.
2. MPI-IO: I/O Extensions to the Message Passing Interface, http://www.mpi-forum.org/docs/mpi-20-html/node172.htm.

order to authorize greater overlap and fault tolerance. These jobs should provide an efficient answer to the requirements of modern parallel applications that are much more consuming and complex than those of the 1990s.

Replacing the Socket interface with MPI in clusters was not the only reason for the leap in parallel computing performance. It was accompanied by the development of dedicated networks that enabled the most to be got out of the advantages of the programming interface by adapting the underlying hardware. Indeed, the specific context of computing clusters – where a closed network (not connected to the Internet) links nodes – the QoS and protocols offered to applications can be adapted.

2.3. Coordination of distributed resources in a grid

2.3.1. *Submission and execution of a distributed application*

Beyond the modifications it imposes on application programming, the use of a distributed infrastructure such as a computing cluster or grid introduces a certain number of new steps:

(1) user authentication enables the system to acquire the user's identity and to grant him or her access to the cluster;

(2) the user enters his or her job-execution request via a portal or directly thanks to a description language specific to each infrastructure. The main languages currently used in computing grids are:

  - Job Submission Description Language (JSDL),
  - Globus Resource Specification Language (RSL),
  - Job Description Language (JDL), and
  - Job Description Language (LDT);

(3) the system allocates resources to the user that match his or her needs;

(4) the authorization mechanisms, generally based on access-control lists, enable the user to create processes on different machines;

(5) each process is composed of one or more control tasks, sharing a similar address space that is created on the machine that was allocated;

(6) during computing, processes can communicate with each other in order to progress with problem solving;

(7) after computing, the results are given directly to the user or are stored in a space chosen by the user during the submission.

A specific process, created when a job is entered, acts on behalf of the user for the entire duration of this job. The mission of this process is to acquire the resources necessary for running the application, depending on the user's rights. On the environment's side, a set of mechanisms and policies must be laid down and activated to enable access, sharing and the use of these resources.

The manager of the cluster or grid, called *middleware*, is in charge of the global management of all of the environment's resources. It is this manager that ensures and coordinates execution of all these steps in direct collaboration with the workflow manager. The role of the middleware (or global operating system) is to hide the system's complexity from applications and provide the abstractions suited to application programming. Functionalities of such an *abstract grid machine* are listed below:

 – security mechanisms management (access control);

 – resource discovery;

 – resource selection and mapping;

 – secured placement of codes and data;

 – running of executables on target machines.

Even if the functionalities required to manage a cluster or grid are roughly the same, the grid, compared to the computing cluster, changes the order of magnitude in terms of:

 – the number of pieces and heterogeneity of *cooperating equipment*;

 – size of *communities* of users; numbers of *interdependent processes*; and also

 – processing, bandwidth and storage *capacities*.

We move from 10 or 100 to 1,000 processors, users, processes. Making this set of remote and heterogeneous hardware and software communicate and cooperate efficiently at these larger scales clearly poses different and complex problems. This is the reason why much of the research, throughout the past decade has centered on grid management and usage issues. More recently, the arrival of mega data centers and cloud computing have raised new technological and scientific challenges to even more impressive scales. Indeed, a data center can contain several hundreds of thousands of machines.

2.3.2. Grid managers

Two large middleware families were put forward to manage grid resources and users:

– Massive grid environments aim to share server clusters that are generally localized in computing centers. The management of these environments can be relatively centralized or slightly decentralized.

– Desktop grid environments enable the use of very widely-spread desktop computers. For example, home PCs connected to the Internet via ADSL links can contribute to the computing platform during their standby period. These environments initially rely on a completely distributed technology, called peer-to-peer or P2P.

Desktop grid technology has shown great benefit for large-scale use in programs such as SETI@home and, at the same time, on a lower scale in business intranets. This is because it allows low-cost deployment. The constraints of this technology are essentially due to the necessary split of executable files and data sets to sizes small enough to be executed on desktop computers. Furthermore, this technology is reserved for applications that can function in a reduced-reliability environment. These applications must be robust so as to avoid security problems linked to execution on unmonitored hardware.

It is OGF[3] that standardizes the roles, architecture and interfaces of massive grid middleware. The main managers are Globus[4] and Unicore[5].

Globus [FOS 97] aims to offer secure remote process running and user-control services at the *network system* level. The performance, control and transparency level offered is relatively low. Nevertheless, large-scale deployment of software such as provided by Globus [FOS 04] and standards such as OGSA [FOS 02] and Web Services Resource Framework within national or international projects (TeraGrid, EU DataGRID, Naregi, NorduGRID, Enabling Grids for E-sciencE and LCG) has enabled large communities of potential users to become familiar with wide-area distributed computing. It is up to us to experiment with and to imagine the benefits of this approach. The designers themselves noticed and identified its main limits: insufficiency and indeterminism of network performance as well as the difficulty in globally securing a distributed infrastructure [VIC 02, MAR 05a]. Thus, over the years new methods, services and protocols have been introduced to remedy this.

2.4. Conclusion

In this chapter, we have seen that the concepts of computer clusters, grids and clouds have been successively developed to respond to an increasing and diversified demand for computing facilities. These different concepts complete rather than oppose each other. Clusters aggregate PCs interconnected by a local network to provide a computing power that is greater than a simple machine, and at a much lower cost than a multiprocessor supercomputer. Grids link heterogeneous resources – often computer clusters – via a WAN to enable several organizations to mutualize their dispersed resources. Clouds, through a paid and secure service, enable the remote and transparent use of

---

3. OGF: The Open Grid Forum, www.ogf.org.

4. Globus toolkit, www.globus.org.

5. Unicore toolkit, www.unicore.org.

clusters or grids composed of rare and/or powerful resources, whether interconnected to each other or not. Furthermore, we have shown that applications being run on these computing infrastructures have different requirements in terms of the performance criteria of communications. In the next chapter, we provide a more precise analysis of the place and constraints of the network within these infrastructures and we present the challenges posed to network technologies to enable computing networks to reach their full potential and their users to receive the greatest benefit from them.

Chapter 3

Specificities of Computing Networks

In the context of computing networks, the network, its protocols and its associated software tools must offer programmers and users efficient interconnection and communication mechanisms between distributed entities. It must also provide simple and quasi-transparent communication and network-monitoring services. These service needs are very different depending on the applications (massively parallel, loosely coupled or collaborative) and environments in which they are executed.

This chapter classifies computing networks, gives an inventory of the performance and service constraints imposed by each context, and studies the limits of traditional protocols with regard to these needs. We will develop the different solutions put forward to address these constraints in later chapters.

3.1. Typology of computing networks

In Chapter 1 we classified distributed computing environments into three large families: clusters, grids and clouds. The main differences between these environments are the characteristics of the aggregated resources, the geographical distribution, and the entity in charge of managing these resources. The central and recurring element of all these environments is the interconnection network, whose main function is to ensure connectivity between resources. Each level of aggregation of physical components has a corresponding network and a set of functions and associated services.

We therefore distinguish between cluster networks, grid networks and cloud networks. It must be noted that there are also networks internal to machines, particularly in multicore architectures or at the very core of these machines' hardware components (known as network on chip or NOC). In this book we do not consider these internal networks, but instead concentrate on the interconnection networks of computing machines. In addition to this, we solely consider wired networks. Nevertheless, the problems and solutions proposed can, in quite a few cases, be extended to the domain of wireless networks.

At the most abstract level, all these networks can be represented by graphs. A graph is a $G = (V, E)$ couple formed from a set of nodes and a finite set of arcs. The machines are the end nodes of this graph. The other nodes, having several arcs, represent the pieces of equipment in the network whose role is to retransmit information from the sender to the receiver. Table 3.1 gives the main attributes of the different networks considered in this book.

Characteristics	Cluster	Grid	Cloud
Type of network	Local	Wide-area	Internet
	Yes	Yes	No
Homogeneous machines	Yes	No	Unknown
Latency	Low	High	High
Throughput	High	High	Low
Type of network protocol	Ethernet or dedicated	IP	IP
Robustness of communications	Yes	Yes	Yes
Predictability of communications	Yes	No	No
Security of communications	Yes	No	No

Table 3.1. *Principal properties of computing networks*

3.1.1. *Cluster networks*

In clusters that aim to offer a low-cost powerful computing environment to applications that are often parallel, the local network and its performances play a dominant role. Applications, aware of the existence of a specific network, try to make the best use of it to maximize their overall performance. Two types of network are used in this context:

– high-performance dedicated networks (see Chapter 4); and

– a very high-speed Ethernet network (1 Gbit/s or 10 Gbit/s). This network serves for inter-process communications and potentially for input/output operations. In computing clusters, it is often doubled with a lower speed, Ethernet-based control network.

3.1.2. *Grid networks*

In grids, the primary goal is to connect heterogeneous equipment via a wide-area network (WAN) to mutualize dispersed resources. The *grid network* is made by interconnecting local cluster networks that aggregate resources on the same site and those that interconnect sites. The grid network is therefore a complex interconnection of heterogeneous networks that can be dedicated. We distinguish three levels in this interconnection:

– the local-area network level;

– the access-link level; and

– the wide-area network level.

Within the various sites of the grid, the local-area network is often based on high-speed Ethernet technology (1 or 10 Gbit/s). To interconnect the remote sites, long-distance links are provided by a network operator. Depending on the service supplied by this operator, the grid will be supported either by provisioned virtual private links based on a technology such as Multi Protocol Label Switching with Traffic Engineering (MPLS-TE) or by dedicated optical links (lambda path). In the case of desktop computer grids, the wide-area network is the Internet.

In current international grids such as the Enabling Grids for E-sciencE or EGEE [EGE 04], local-area networks are typically high-speed packet-switching Ethernet networks (1 or 10 Gbit/s). In the Grid5000 [BOL 06b], local-area networks are 1 or 10 Gbit/s Ethernet networks are doubled with dedicated high-performance networks. Access links are 10 Gbit/s. In research grids, virtual private links are supplied by national research and education networks, such as France's National Telecommunication Network for Technology, Education and Research (RENATER) for Grid5000, or the pan European data communications network, GEANT, for EGI.

In order to profit as much as possible from these infrastructures, it is necessary to share the network between the different grid users while providing an abundant bandwidth for each application. Whether over the Internet or a private network, the critical issue is sharing the capacity of the site's link to the wide-area network. The bottleneck is generally located at this level. Figure 3.1, which represents the structure of the interconnection network of the Grid5000 platform, highlights the strong aggregation at the level of the access points to the wide-area network. The individual capacity of each machine connected to the grid is of the same order of magnitude as the access link (for example 1 or 10 Gbit/s). The rate of aggregation, K, is the ratio of the uplink capacity, C_{access}, and total capacity of the source, C_{source}. $K = C_{access}/C_{source}$ at the access point. In the Internet, this rate of aggregation is in the order of 1,000 or 10,000. Indeed, for an Internet provider with an access link of the order of 1 Gbit/s, the machine's throughput or that of the client's ADSL link is in the order of 10 Mbit/s. In a grid, this rate is 1 or 10. The rate of potential congestion at the point of access, CP, defined by $CP = n * C_{source}/C_{access} = n/K$, is therefore inversely proportional to the rate of aggregation. CP increases linearly with the number of local machines simultaneously trying to communicate with one of the grid's external machines. This rate of potential congestion very quickly exceeds the critical value of 1, which expresses congestion if all the machines simultaneously communicate in the middle of the operation.

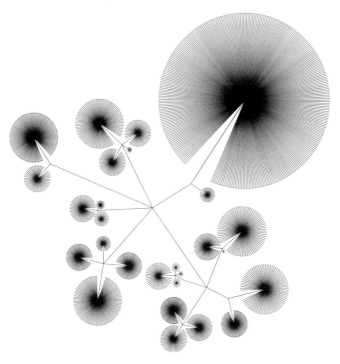

Figure 3.1. *Model of the Grid5000's core network*

To access remote computers or files, distributed applications use the standard communication interface and protocols of current operating systems: Transport Control Protocol (TCP)/Internet Protocol (IP) sockets and protocols.

3.1.3. *Computing cloud networks*

In the case of cloud computing, computer access remote and is even more transparent than in grids. Users connect to the cloud through a web portal and all exchanges with the allocated resources are done via the user's Internet link. Data and codes are sent to available remote machines and can be co-localized there. Applications are not informed of the nature and distribution of resources that are attributed to them and therefore cannot optimize communications between processes. Each program is supposed to be executed autonomously on a computer or an independent virtual machine. The cloud service takes charge of all the potential transfers between machines. The programming model is still very simple but could become more complex in the future if cloud technology spreads more widely.

3.2. Network transparency

3.2.1. *The advantages of transparency*

Grids are characterized by:

– a significant heterogeneity of the aggregation resources and their interconnection networks;

– the strong dynamic of these resources and networks;

– a large diversity of needs and often a difficulty in specifying them;

– a high need for performance that is often at the limits of the hardware's capacity;

– an intense load variability;

– a multi-domain context (private, public);

– multiple policies (multi-user, multiple organizations);

– varied and potentially multipoint communication schemes (multicast, all-to-all, etc.).

One of the main objectives of grid software was to make all of these factors, and the network in particular, as transparent as possible to users. Let us note that this objective has characterized distributed systems since the beginning of the 1990s. In the very heterogeneous and multi-domain context of grids, this objective is even more important.

Programming applications on such systems can be very complicated. Programming on a grid adds new levels of complexity compared to programming a parallel application, which requires specific expertise to start with. Parallel-programming approaches based on message communication libraries, such as the Message-Passing Interface or MPI, require the programmer to explicitly describe communications between processes. Distributed systems and grids additionally require the software interfaces to be remotely accessible through unreliable and nondeterministic network connections. Ideally, such access should thus be transparent, i.e. connections should not be explicitly described by the programmer. The gap separating the system from the application programmer increases when going from parallel systems to distributed systems to grids.

To enable the programming and execution of a distributed application, the network and communication tools must offer basic functions, such as connection, sending and receiving of messages or files. Thus, to create and use a complex aggregation of widely-distributed resources and have basic communication functionalities, communities of middleware designers and grid-application programmers naturally relied on the Internet's packet-switching technology. Indeed, this technology addresses interoperability demands, masks equipment and technology heterogeneity, and shows robustness and scalability properties. Furthermore, to send messages or files, applications distributed on a grid use the TCP or User Datagram Protocol (UDP). Both of these protocols are widely diffused and available on computing nodes, and enable communication over both short- and long-distance links. Thus, in the grids deployed and used today, the network is transparent and the protocols used inherit the same characteristics as those of the Internet.

3.2.2. *Foundations of network transparency*

To mask network heterogeneity, the International Organization for Standardization proposed the Open Systems Interconnection or OSI model; see Figure 3.2. This is a model of open-systems interconnection that has been a reference for 40 years.

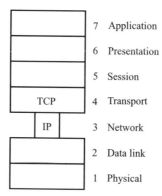

Figure 3.2. *The International Organization for Standardization's OSI model*

This model defines seven layers, each providing a specific service. For example, the data-link layer (level 2) provides the service enabling access and control when sharing the physical medium. In this model, a level-N layer solely calls on the layer immediately below[1] and data pass from one layer to the next, while being encapsulated (i.e. each layer only adds the necessary headers for service management at its level to the above level's data). This model was used and simplified in the TCP/IP Internet protocol architecture that governs all communications on the planet.

The fourth layer, the transport layer, is very important because it is the first level that has an end-to-end view of the network. It is this layer that provides the means of communication between two application processes. Its role is to ensure that information is transported from one end of the network to the other, correcting possible errors introduced by network elements. The most well-known and frequently used transport protocol is TCP. This is the same TCP of the Internet's TCP/IP architecture represented in Figure 3.3. Studies have shown that

1. This isolation can pose problems, since some useful information is not brought back up to the upper layers. This, for example, can lead to the model not being able to distinguish a loss due to corruption from a loss due to congestion.

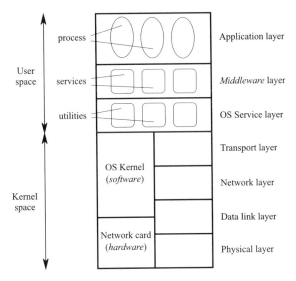

Figure 3.3. *Protocol layer stack*

80–95% of the Internet's current traffic is made up of TCP streams. This success is due to the presence of this protocol in all the major operating systems and to the fact that free implementation has been available since the time the protocol was introduced. The following list presents a few of the TCP's main properties:

(1) reliability: TCP is in charge of packet-routing and ensures the integrity of such packets;

(2) scalability capacity: TCP is used by almost all of the Internet's end hosts (billions of machines);

(3) stability: regardless of disturbances, TCP ensures the system's convergence towards stable and efficient operation;

(4) robustness: TCP can function in extreme conditions of loss rate and latency;

(5) fair sharing: TCP enables different users to have a proportional part of the bandwidth.

TCP enables a connection to be established with a destination from a source by enabling them to agree on a sequence number (a three-way handshake), which counts the number of bytes sent by the source. The destination returns packets containing a sequence number, which correspond to the acknowledgement of the highest continuous-sequence number received. This mechanism allows reliable data forwarding (i.e. it means that it is possible to detect the loss of packets).

A TCP connection is identified by a digit couple, a source port and a destination port, enabling the process to clearly identify (by adding the IP address couple) what it is trying to communicate with. Data are transmitted and received across Sockets, which are the logical entities representing the endpoints of the *pipe*.

3.2.3. *The limits of TCP and IP in clusters*

IP networks were invented at the end of the 1970s. Even though a few optimizations have been carried out since, the implementation of TCP/IP layers in modern operating systems is based on the same principles. Figure 3.4 presents the different layers of the network-access software in the UNIX system.

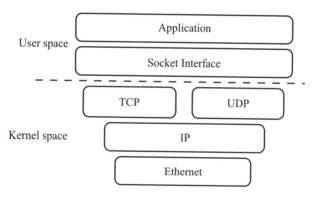

Figure 3.4. *Access to Ethernet networks through the TCP and UDP protocols and the Socket interface*

Applications communicate through the Socket interface, which enables access to a reliable and connected transport service – TCP – and to an unreliable and unconnected transport service – UDP. These two services are implemented by the protocols of the same name and take charge of high-level data transmission between remote applications. The IP layer carries out packet-routing across various types of intermediary equipment (routers and gateways) up to the receiver. Finally, the link-level layer, typically Ethernet in local-area networks, is in charge of packet-transmission on the physical link using frames. This layered model allows many advanced functionalities that are unfortunately not very interesting in computing clusters because routing is often useless in them, whereas retransmission and congestion control are much more important.

The network-access Socket interface offers a syntax of the same type as the UNIX file-access interface. Upon sending, the system copies the data in a special area (the Socket buffer) then returns to the application; see Figure 3.5. The operating system is then in charge of sending the data in the background from this area to the network interface card through direct memory access. Thus, the application is only blocked during copying, instead of having to wait for the last acknowledgement message of the last packet to be received (which can take a long time if the receiver is on the other side of the world). On reception, the strategy is symmetrical but the receiver is blocked until data arrives in the user memory. This communication model is synchronous and even if non-blocking variations exist the application cannot truly work during communication processing.

This model also has the drawback of being demanding in processing time and memory-bus occupation. (There are three accesses on the sender's end and three on the receiver's end.) This is because a memory copy must be created upon sending and receiving. Furthermore, stacking different protocols is quite cumbersome because they each add their header to the packets and require the computation of checksums to verify data integrity. High-speed communications will therefore consume a very large quantity of processing time. For

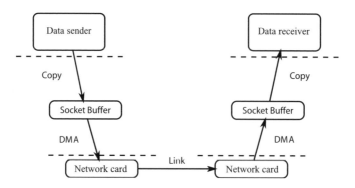

Figure 3.5. *Data transfer using the socket interface*

example, the protocol processing of a 10 Gbit/s connection saturates a modern processor's core. In addition, these protocol processes increase communication latency. This model's ability to provide fast notifications of network events (data reception or sending termination) is limited. Indeed, when simultaneous communications have been sent to numerous nodes, the Socket interface requires the explicit verification of the state of each connection to determine whether the data have arrived. The classic event notification strategy (poll/select) turned out to be unable to efficiently handle a large number of connections. The results of the research carried out for the web servers can also be applied to large computing systems. This was reflected by new variations of poll, enabling sources of interest to be recorded [BAN 99]. The new variations of poll eventually appeared in operating systems, first with k_{event}/k_{queue} in FreeBSD, then with epoll in Linux. Other works considered using threads to process these network events. Threads were not designed for highly *event-based* applications but rather for applications necessitating a real concurrence between execution queues [OUS 96]. The compromise consisting of distributing the sources of events across a certain number of threads has, however, proved its efficiency[2]. These new implementations have enabled applications to be scaled to large distributed systems by efficiently handling network communications to a very large number of machines. Event notification still suffers from a significant latency, however, notably because of the system-call necessary to access network events.

3.2.4. *Limits of TCP and network transparency in grids*

The Internet's best-effort service provides the ubiquitous connectivity necessary and allows abstraction from the high heterogeneity of interconnection. The level of abstraction and service supplied by the TCP and IP, however, does not enable efficient execution of applications. Thus, whereas functional transparency *vis-à-vis* programming is very noticeable, there is no transparency in performance. Moreover, providing a sufficient throughput from one end of the distributed computing environment to the other is a major challenge in ensuring that the global computing system is efficient and fluid. Moving a volume of one terabyte from one end of a European grid to the other can take more than a week when the average speed of network links is 10 Mbit/s (the typical speed of an ADSL link). If it is a dedicated 1 Gbit/s network, the transfer time will only be a few hours.

3.2.5. *TCP in a high bandwidth-delay product network*

Delivering high-performance communications in a high-bandwidth delay-product network is a significant challenge for a simple point-to-point communication. The Internet's traditional transport protocol, TCP, as well as its variations were developed for shared networks in which link bandwidth is a critical resource. Therefore, congestion-control mechanisms, aiming to manage internal contention, try to find the correct balance between competition that is not too aggressive and acceptable end-to-end performance. A slow-start therefore forces TCP to wait a long time before reaching maximum

---

2. Input/output event handling under Linux, www.atnf.csiro.au/people/rgooch/linux/docs/io-events.html.

speed when the distance between the sender and receiver is significant. There is also a considerable delay in reaching maximum speed after packet loss. In a network in which internal congestion events are rare, the problem of speed and congestion control moves to the endpoints (or access links), which become bottlenecks. Furthermore, in a multipoint context where streams can have variable bandwidth-delay products, the allocation of throughput between streams is not fair. We study these high-speed transfer problems in Chapter 5.

3.2.6. *Limits of the absence of communication control*

The generalized use of the TCP in a grid ensures equitable sharing of overall bandwidth and that of access links in particular. Nevertheless, such an approach does not guarantee a minimum throughput. Variability in load-performance is not always suitable for the user's objective of performance, which is to minimize the total execution time of applications. A simple connectivity service is therefore neither sufficient nor satisfactory.

The performance of application execution is largely determined by the movements of data. With the TCP/IP approach, it is difficult to predict and obtain in practice. The possibility of message loss, significant and variable transmission delays, and the dynamic behavior of links between remote processes are a significant challenge for the models and techniques developed in the context of parallel and distributed computing on computing clusters. Consequently, whereas several grids exist today and are used daily, such as the EGEE [EGE 04], it is commonly admitted that they are far from being easy to use technological platforms. They are not sufficiently robust and do not provide a high enough performance to serve the needs of each application scenario. This is because of the characteristics of the communications protocols used.

To increase performance, application programmers therefore seek to distinguish between local-area and wide-area communications. In the second generation of grids, middleware is also equipped with network-monitoring and measurement functionalities. Applications or services can consequently monitor network load and optimize their performance by being based on predictions offered by environments of network-performance measurement and estimation, such as NWS (Network Weather Service) systems [WOL 99].

This approach causes the level of complexity of programming applications on a grid to increase for the following reasons:

– computing resources are heterogeneous in terms of architecture as well as performance;

– network resources are very heterogeneous in terms of bandwidth and latency, in space and in time;

– as each part of a distributed application generally depends on one or more other parts, a non-optimal allocation of tasks to servers can lead to long processing delays. To get good performance, task sequencing on resources has become more complex.

Today, distributed applications can monitor the network's state. The network itself still remains unaware of the constraints of the applications that are executed, however, and does not provide specific bandwidth services or quality of service (QoS). In Chapter 6, we will see that the technological advances in optical networks offer new dynamic services that are very interesting for grids. The challenge is to make the ever-increasing capacities and the increasingly sophisticated services supplied by the optical network infrastructures accessible to middleware and applications. For this, the global cloud network must be considered a resource in and by itself, and its sharing mode must be globally controlled. The performance, security and functionalities must be rendered deterministic and compatible with computing algorithms.

In summary, the grid context, and by extension that of very large-scale computing, is very different from that of the traditional Internet, for which the TCP and IP were designed. This is because:

– control over latencies and throughputs is critical for the global performance of infrastructure and applications;

– certain communications can tolerate packet losses and do not systematically require messages to occur in a specific order;

– the models of cooperation between remote entities are multipoint (of the N-N type) rather than point-to-point (of the 1-1 type), as in the client-server mode on which the main Internet applications are based;

– the communication paths between remote processes are very hierarchically structured, with some the nodes of the interconnection graph having a very high density. These nodes correspond to aggregation points bordering the wide-area network and are therefore often susceptible to congestion;

– control over resource usage is important to be able to develop a solid economical model;

– trust domains must be well delimited, and this must occur in a dynamic way.

3.3. Detailed analysis of characteristics expected from protocols

The classification of grid applications presented in Chapter 2 highlighted comparatively strong locality and performance (QoS) criteria, which are directly linked to the network. The analysis of applications according to this classification showed that network needs are different depending on the application's phases (preparation, execution, post-processing). Throughput performance (low latency), needs are more demanding during execution phases, in which costly resources (computing, instruments and users) are simultaneously active and tightly coupled. Phases of exchanges with storage spaces are more demanding in bandwidth but more relaxed in delay constraints. The design and composition constraints of a grid's network and protocols depend on topological criteria (number of sites, number of users and localization constraints) and on performance criteria (degree of coupling of targeted applications that directly influence the traditional QoS parameters: throughput, delay, reliability and robustness).

3.3.1. *Topological criteria*

3.3.1.1. *Number of sites involved*

Two typical organizations can be distinguished regarding interactions between the processes making up a distributed application.

In the first type, *single-site* applications do not use the network during the execution phase. Only the initialization, input data transfer, or result recovery and termination phases use the network. This organization is present in local simulations on computing grids. On the one hand, the network's performance needs in terms of delay are less critical than during the execution phase; on the other hand, bandwidth needs can be very significant.

The other type of organization is called *multi-site*. In this, processes interact more during execution. For certain simulations, synchronization between processes is required at each iteration step. This stronger coupling between processes requires a stable network capacity throughout execution. In the case of remote visualization, the need for interactivity is very strong. Multi-site applications can display simple virtual topologies (chain of resources, as in the pipeline case) or more complex ones (in the case of distributed computing on several randomly chosen sites).

3.3.1.2. *Number of users involved*

The number of users is another topological criterion. Single-user applications are typically computing applications in which a single user runs the application and waits for the results. Multi-user applications are those that offer the possibility of collaborative work. This second type needs a high level of interactivity, and therefore a high level of connectivity with all the users who interact in real time through the application.

3.3.1.3. *Resource-localization constraints*

The possibility of choosing the location of a resource influences the interconnection's composition constraints. Data-acquisition (sensor networks) or visualization instruments are by nature often very localized, as for example in the case of a medical imaging application such as the one displayed in Figure 3.6. Storage spaces or even data-based resources, however, have more flexible constraints with regards to location. Finally, computing resources are very often generic. As with users they are localized as in the case of a fixed-network connection, or mobile, as in the case of a radio-network connection. Collaborative multi-site applications provide the greatest constraint for composing a connection graph.

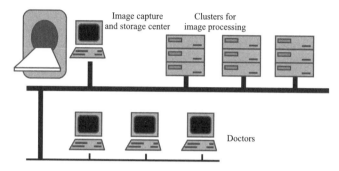

Figure 3.6. *Distribution of entities in a medical-imagery application displayed on a grid*

3.3.2. *Performance criteria*

3.3.2.1. *Degree of inter-task coupling*

It is the degree of inter-task synchronization and coupling that defines the application's sensitivity to communication latency. Returning to the classification in Chapter 2, applications of the resource-sharing class often need to synchronize computing phases and exchange data during execution. Data updating can be controlled by distributed file systems, with competition control done by transactions or any other technique/algorithm that is used to solve the problem of multiple write access to a shared resource, such as software locks. These applications do not have interactivity constraints. They show a variable level of coupling between processes, which can influence the choice of resources (whether they must be near each other or not, for example). Scheduling needs are low once the tasks have been allocated to the resources, but the placement can be requested at very short-term intervals, imposing a certain degree of reactivity to the allocation process. The requesting of resources can take place in advance, from the moment users plan their load needs (this can be automated by heuristics, time series, etc.).

In the class of high-performance distributed computing applications, two degrees of coupling are found:

– loose coupling exists between various long computing phases, between which large quantities of data need to be transferred;

– tight coupling exists in each long phase, where several parallel execution streams cooperate by sharing data space between computing resources.

This cooperation is also done in stages, where data coherence occurs; generally via exchanges on the space sharing's borders. These applications therefore require synchronizations, which are generally associated with (large and small) data exchanges. These synchronizations do not have real-time constraints, however, and the next step can be started as soon as data from the neighbors or from the phase before have arrived.

To avoid resource idleness, it is a good thing to orchestrate the execution of cooperating phases in such a way as to make them progress at the same speed. Determining the duration of the phases can enable better reservation of the network. From the point of view of interactivity, distributed-computing applications have little interactivity requirements. In this application class, the needs identified are the transfers of large amounts of data, burst transfers and workflow management.

3.3.2.2. *Sensitivity to latency and throughput*

Each application class presented in Chapter 2 exhibits different delay, throughput, reliability and robustness needs. In the group of distributed parallel computing applications, tasks calculate more data and the interaction is fine-grained. Sensitivity to latency is therefore very high. In contrast to the case of distributed parallel computing, high-speed computing tasks do not communicate with each other (or they communicate little). Their throughput needs, for computing preparation and data routing, can be significant. For on-demand computing, tasks are allocated to any of the computers based on specific criteria. It is difficult to evaluate throughput- or delay-sensitivity. These metrics, without being critical, influence the overall performance of the system and the degree of user satisfaction. For the group of data-intensive applications, complexity lies in the combined allocation of several tasks as well as in the availability of data.

Class E applications aggregate a certain number of users who wish to simultaneously modify the virtual space where they collaborate. These applications are very sensitive to latency. Applications belonging to the cooperation and visualization class require high network reactivity. Updates must be done in real time so as not to compromise the visualization. Some can tolerate reductions in quality. With critical data paths it is necessary to guarantee that the computations carried out remotely quickly become visible. It does seem possible, however, to determine the throughput necessary for a given resolution at a given frame rate with data from a known origin.

In collaborative-work applications, several users on different sites interact. Remote visualization is a simplification of collaborative work where a single user operates on the data. The application's role is often to develop complex projects, such as in the automobile industry and the electronics or environment domains. Users participate in real time and modify the state of the project. These modifications must have an immediate effect on the project that is visible to the other users. It is necessary to have a multipoint communication. Latency must ideally remain in the order of one millisecond and the network must guarantee a certain throughput for each user, possibly rented on an on-demand basis. Some applications require distributed archive systems due to the volume of data manipulated or to act as a local cache for the visualized data.

To conclude this study of application classes, we note that only distributed parallel computing and collaborative computing use the network during the execution phases; the other application classes do not. These two application classes will be the most sensitive to latency. In addition, distributed parallel computing requires communications to be 100% reliable, unlike collaborative computing.

3.3.2.3. *Sensitivity to throughput and its control*

Applications for high-speed computing, on-demand computing and data-intensive computing should work on local data. The implementation of these applications must therefore guarantee that the data are locally present or that remote access is efficient. This implies a high demand in throughput during the preparation and post-processing phases. It is not necessary to guarantee a high level of service, however, for the communication streams.

The transfer time, T, of a volume of data, V, from one point to another is expressed, in a simplified way, by: $T = V/r + d$ where r is the actual end-to-end throughput between the two communicating processes, and d the end-to-end delay. d is a very complex sum of variable and fixed delays depending directly on the network's load at time t, whereas r is the sample minimum of the throughput of each of the path's numerous segments. Depending on whether V will be very big or very small, factors r or d will be dominant. In addition to the intrinsic value of r or d, their variability can also be very detrimental to a computing application or to the distributed system as a whole. This variability depends directly on the interactions between the streams internal and external to the grid.

Grid technologies facilitate resource allocation to multiple applications running simultaneously. The activities associated with a user or an organization can therefore influence the performance seen by other processes being executed on the same platform. The problem is in providing tools for control or even performance isolation. One of the most significant problems currently faced by grid communities is that, although they provide access to several heterogeneous resources, the available ones seldom meet the needs of a specific application or service. In an environment where resource availability and software demands quickly increase, it is possible to end up with:

– a suboptimal use of resources;

– user frustration; or

– efforts wasted trying to establish connections between the applications and resources.

It is therefore desirable that grids meet the needs in terms of network QoS and performance control, in addition to meeting those related to access to diverse, rare and powerful resources.

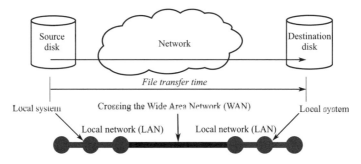

Figure 3.7. *Cost of file transfer in a grid: local and system costs must be added to the cost of wide-area network feed-through*

Figure 3.7 illustrates the different networks crossed during a file transfer. The QoS and performances of each one of these segments must be carefully examined to maximize the performance of the transfer.

3.3.2.4. *Sensitivity to confidentiality and security*

Applications created for industrial purposes have strong concerns regarding confidentiality. They require secure connections, to the point that they prevent the application from being deployed outside the company's grounds. The aspect of security is fundamental, especially when a business must run its application on several sites or an external site. A secure network is necessary not only to keep communications secret but also to ensure controlled access to end resources.

3.3.2.5. *Summary of requirements*

Most applications would benefit from a high-performance (very low latency) network to achieve better results, but only the strongly synchronized applications are particularly sensitive to it. Some applications can have particular security (encrypted channels) and interactivity requirements. The majority of applications need a high transfer rate, particularly to access data sources and results. Finally, distributed applications on grids could benefit from functionalities, such as advanced reservation and (possibly secured) deterministic scheduling of network transfers. The discovery of network capacity, monitoring of service level, synchronization of communication and computing, negotiation of bandwidth and performant transport protocols are functionalities capable of improving grid usage.

This analysis shows that the description of the application's behavior is necessary to allow an easier and more informed choice about the network and the communication protocols to be used. Ideally, it is the workflow that should incorporate information on inter-task communications, specifying the deadline, volume, direction, profile or quality desired. In general, the workflow does not give this explicit description. Means for automatically obtaining or predicting this description should be provided.

3.4. Conclusion

In this chapter we identified four main challenges related to the interconnection network and protocols in order to support network computing applications:

– latency;
– distance;
– throughput; and
– security.

Of course, other challenges face networks and protocols in the context of an increasingly massive deployment of grid and cloud-computing technologies:

– the integration of wireless networks and mobility;
– the dynamicity of links and resources;

– robustness and fault-tolerance; and

– the definition of a *viable* economic model.

It is fundamental to ensure that the considerable potential offered by resource aggregation does not remain unexploited, or even wasted, because of the inadequacy of the communication models and mechanisms implemented. Recent technological evolutions give a glimpse of a large number of new solutions just waiting to be exploited. It is these proposed evolutions and software solutions that we develop in the rest of this book. We attempt to show how these new approaches address the four main challenges: latency, distance, throughput and security.

We study the specific problem of cluster networks in Chapter 4. In that chapter, we specifically analyze the constraints of grid networks. We develop the related issues of throughput and distance in Chapter 5. In Chapter 6 we examine performance monitoring.

In Chapter 7, we study the various optical technologies that address the need for very high throughputs. In Chapter 8, we show how a bandwidth-on-demand service allows us to offer a controlled very-high throughput for a limited period of time. The chapter deals with the issues of communication- and access-security in a distributed computing network. Chapter 10 gives a short guide for tuning your network and end protocols.

Chapter 4

The Challenge of Latency in Computing Clusters

The aim of this chapter is to present the key principles of high-performance networks of computing clusters, their associated protocols and their actual implementation in the operating system (OS) and the hardware.

The specific needs of parallel computing applications in the 1990s led to the development of research on specific networks, protocols and programming interfaces that are much more performant than the traditional technologies. The bandwidth of these high-performance networks has long exceeded 10 Gbit/s, whereas latency easily reaches a few microseconds. Whereas in a traditional Ethernet-type network bandwidth can now reach comparable values, latency still remains significantly longer than a microsecond, which is limiting for very high-performance computing.

The design of these new networks relies on a deep modification of the system and hardware layers in order to facilitate data transfer between user processes.

Indeed, the quality of service (QoS) provided by these networks was designed specifically for the needs of parallel applications in computing clusters, allowing protocols to be closely adapted to them.

In this chapter, we define the key principles of computer-cluster networks and then detail the specific software mechanisms that were introduced in this high-performance context. Finally, we present the different high-performance network technologies introduced over the last 15 years to interconnect the different computers making up a cluster. It must be noted that the principles, software mechanisms and technological innovations exposed in this chapter have been re-used in other, less-demanding contexts, particularly high-speed Ethernet networks, as we show at the end of this chapter.

4.1. Key principles of high-performance networks for clusters

The communication needs of parallel applications being very particular, highly specific networks and protocols were invented for this context. The general idea is to reduce the latency introduced by the network and its protocols. It is done by shortening, as much as possible, the critical path followed by the data exchanged between two processes that are being executed on different nodes. To do this, the specificities of the context and of the programming interface used (Message Passing Interface or MPI) are taken into consideration to suppress costly steps that are useless here. The main mechanisms proposed are:

(1) *Zero-copy communications*: parallel applications should not waste processing time on communications. It is possible to suppress the intermediate copies, which consume a lot of processing time using an interface card capable of initiating direct memory access (DMA) to directly transfer data between the applications' user memory and the network, without using the central processor.

(2) *Removing the OS from the critical path*: the cost of a system call is in the order of a few hundreds of nanoseconds on modern machines. It is possible to avoid system calls (OSbypass) by authorizing applications to directly access the network interface card. The gain in latency is

noticeable, since latencies are of a similar order of magnitude (a few microseconds).

(3) *Reactivity to events*: peripheral devices can notify the central processor of a network event by interrupting it. The cost of an interruption being quite high (several microseconds), however, polling enables faster recovery of events. The counterpart is that polling consumes processing time. Clever mixing of polling (for early-arriving events) and interrupts (for late-arriving events) enables all network events to be recovered with a good balance between reactivity and processor consumption [MAQ 96].

(4) *Protocol processing in the interface card*: the simplicity of the protocol specifically designed for computing clusters enables interface cards equipped with on-board processor and memory to process part or all of it. The application submits its communication requests to the card and then the card handles them in the background while the application can overlap the processing with computation.

(5) *Reliable physical network*: cluster topologies are static and closed and traffic is quite deterministic therein. It is therefore possible to anticipate the quantity of data that can circulate in the different links. Sufficient dimensioning of the network core enables congestion, and therefore loss of messages, to be avoided. In addition, the short length and the reliability of physical links prevent data corruption. Transmission (and retransmission in the case of error) protocols are therefore much less complex and costly than those found in the Internet (Transmission Control Protocol/Internet Protocolor TCP/IP), which is in essence an unreliable and highly congested network. The protocol can therefore be optimized for the errorless case, while error processing can be slow because it is very rarely used.

(6) Source routing: cluster networks are regular and static, allowing routing to be fixed. The processor embedded in the interface card can place routing information at the start of the packet. The role of switches is then reduced to extracting this small header and then directing the packet, which improves performance. Congestion can be managed using very simple flow control at the data-link level, which enables a receiver to inform the sender that it must wait before sending the next packets.

4.2. Software support for high-performance networks

We now detail the different software innovations that enable parallel applications to have excellent performance thanks to MPI implementations on high-performance networks.

4.2.1. *Zero-copy transfers*

The first innovation linked to high-performance networks is the possibility of transferring data directly between the application and the network without intermediate memory-copy like in regular layers, such as TCP/IP. These so-called zero-copy data transfers have the advantage of not using the central processor to carry out a memory copy, which would be very costly for large messages (it takes about one millisecond to copy a megabyte). Zero-copy is implemented by data transfers through DMA, see Figure 4.1. It is initiated by the peripheral device from or to the machine's central memory. In addition to this, modern network cards are capable of computing checksums to verify data integrity: data can be directly transferred through DMA without requiring intervention from the OS. Therefore, it is now possible to saturate physical links, i.e. reaching more than 1 GB/s these days, without saturating the central processor because of copies or checksum computations (The bandwidth of the common Peripheral Component Interconnect or PCI Express buses and the links of the most advanced network technology is 1 GB/s.).

These DMAs have the disadvantage of having significant initialization and termination costs, because it is necessary to give the peripheral device the target memory addresses in advance. DMA must therefore only be used when a sufficient quantity of data must be transferred, typically at least 10 KB.

4.2.2. *OS-bypass*

The second innovation of high-performance networks concerns small messages. Whereas zero-copy communications are preferred for large messages, this is not the case for small messages where latency

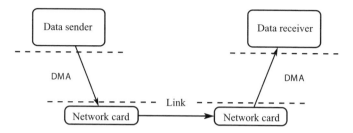

Figure 4.1. *Zero-copy data transfer on a cluster network*

is crucial, and currently reaches about 1 microsecond. Indeed, for a latency d and a bandwidth r, the transfer time of a message of size V is $T = V/r + d$. Since here, d is in the order of the microsecond and r in the order of 1 gigabyte per second, $T \simeq d$ for V in the order of 1 KB.

The initialization cost of a DMA is a few hundred nanoseconds, which is too high compared to the communication's global latency. For small messages it is necessary to shorten the path between the sending application and its target on another node by as much as possible. This is achieved by shortening all of the steps, particularly the transfers between the application and the peripheral device.

To do so, a novel idea was proposed to take the OS out of the critical path, i.e. directly submitting requests to the card from applications in the user space (OS-bypass). Indeed, the cost of a system call has long been in the order of 1 microsecond, which has greatly limited latency reduction. Techniques for projecting the peripheral devices' resources into the applications' memory have been used, so that the latter has been able to write commands directly in the former, using programmed input/output (PIO), which is the processor writing in the resources of a peripheral device. This requires the OS to work during initialization but considerably simplifies things later on.

4.2.3. *Event notification*

In the same way that the OS is avoided during sending in order to reduce latency, it can also be avoided during event notification when receiving. The peripheral device will put events directly in the application's memory space. The application can then scan the designated memory area to immediately obtain these events. The duration of polling is of the same order of magnitude as network latency, which is very low in this instance. This polling therefore does not last very long and is not costly for the application. This waste of a few processing cycles enables very low end-to-end latencies to be achieved for small messages thanks to fast notification without paying the prohibitive extra cost of an interrupt (several microseconds).

For big messages, during the DMA's termination, it is also necessary for the peripheral device to be able to notify the application when it reaches the end of its job. This requires either an explicit interruption of the central processor by the peripheral device or, conversely, active polling of the peripheral device by the processor. With the cost of interrupts of a few microseconds being negligible compared to the transfer time of a message of several dozen kilobytes, this strategy is often preferred.

Fast notification of the termination of requests is an important point in the design of high-performance networks. In fact, the techniques used mix polling, for early notifications (the application does the polling), and interrupts for late notifications (the application sleeps and is awoken by an interrupt from the network card). These mechanisms allow the quick notification of an application that has requested to be blocked until a request is terminated.

Furthermore, it can be important to notify the application without it being forced to interrupt computing to explicitly request the status of on-going requests. Most programming interfaces for fast networks only make communications progress when the application explicitly calls a library function. It is sometimes desirable, however, to process tasks in the background without waiting for the application to intervene, for example to release resources or answer a remote request, such as a *rendezvous* request. To do this, the active messages (AM) [EIC 92] programming interface uses a special thread in charge of calling the routines (receive handler) for processing the messages received.

Therefore, instead of only allowing communications to progress when the application calls library functions, exchanges continue continuously in the background. This further enables us to improve the overlap of communications by computing because the application can concentrate on the latter. The Myricom MX communication library also uses a strategy like this to process *rendezvous* and connections in the background.

These notification methods are effective but are considerably different from standard strategies, such as *poll/select* or – more recently in Linux – *epoll*. Indeed, the latter two are explicitly handled by the OS that is in charge of manipulating several sources, advancing in the background, etc. They have enabled applications to efficiently wait for network events (in particular the arrival of messages in TCP or User Datagram Protocol or UDP connections) without being impacted by the number of sources that must be listened to simultaneously. This model is quite different from user-space notifications in libraries managing fast networks, which makes their joint use very difficult. For example, it is impossible to uniformly receive events from high-performance networks and from the discs, which can reduce the efficiency of a distributed storage server.

4.2.4. *The problem of address translation*

The application's direct submission (using OS bypass) of requests involving DMA between the application's memory and the network has raised a rather new technical problem. Generally the application only uses virtual addresses, whereas the hardware only uses physical addresses. Translation is normally carried out in the OS: the application passes virtual addresses to the kernel using a system call and then the kernel translates them into physical addresses before giving them to the hardware.

In high-performance networks, OS bypass communications avoid the OS in order to reduce latency. This therefore prevents the OS from helping to translate addresses. The most widespread strategy for solving this problem is called *memory registration*. This consists of declaring the memory areas that will be used in communications during initialization. A system call is then made to translate the memory addresses and permanently register the correspondence in the interface card (see Figure 4.2(a)). All communications can then be OS bypass, with the application passing virtual addresses to the card and the card translating them using the pre-registered correspondences (Figure 4.2(b)). This idea was first introduced in research on the U-Net system [EIC 95] in the form of a statically pre-registered zone. It was then generalized in the U-Net/MM system [WEL 97].

Memory registration is an effective method but it has two significant drawbacks. First, applications are not usually written to adequately prepare the memory areas used for input/output (I/O) operations. Using such a model in a normal application can therefore be difficult. One commonly used solution consists of putting a shared library in charge of on-the-fly and transparent registration of the memory areas used by the application in its I/O operations.

The second problem is the often very high cost of registering and deregistering memory, which can be in the order of 100 microseconds. This cost is notably much higher than the latency of small messages (a few microseconds). It is therefore only profitable if the memory areas are large and/or re-used several times. For small messages, it remains preferable to use an intermediate copy in a statically pre-registered memory area. Wasting a few processor cycles is, in the end, more economical than registering.

In other cases, a strategy called recording *memory cache* [TEZ 98] is used. Rather than deregistering a memory area from the moment the communication it was involved in is terminated, deregistration of memory areas is slowed down by as much as possible. Indeed, as long as it is possible to record new pages, it is useless to waste time deregistering old ones. The cost of actual deregistration is therefore avoided. In addition, if an area is left registered in the cache, its subsequent re-uses will not require new registration. The overall cost

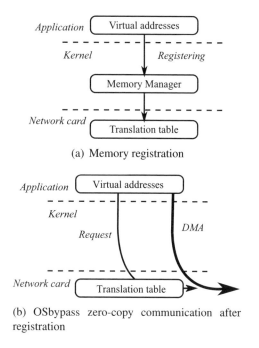

(a) Memory registration

(b) OSbypass zero-copy communication after registration

Figure 4.2. *OSbypass zero-copy model with memory registration*

is therefore greatly reduced, particularly if the same memory areas are re-used several times.

This effective strategy poses many technical problems related to detecting areas kept registered when the application has released them. It is necessary to be able to keep the cache up-to-date with the modifications of the application's addressing space, which is generally difficult. Works have been proposed to modify the OS to this end [GOG 04]. A similar implementation should be integrated in the Linux kernel in the near future.

4.2.5. *Non-blocking programming models*

Support for zero-copy communications and OS bypass relies on the card, not the OS, processing communication requests by the card and not by the OS. This idea enables non-blocking programming models to be implemented.

The application submits requests to the card, overlaps their processing with computations, and then tests their termination later on. These requests come in two types, which correspond to the two programming paradigms for parallel application:

– *message passing*; and

– *remote memory-access.*

4.2.5.1. *Case 1: message-passing*

In the first case, requests are of the message-sending and -receiving type, like in MPI. The parameters of these requests are compared to find out which sending will be received by which receiving request. This matching can be carried out in the host (which reduces recovery) or in the interface card (which can necessitate a lot of memory and on-board power resources).

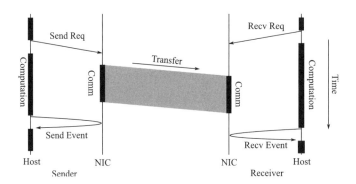

Figure 4.3. *Time diagram of a communication based on the message-passing paradigm. The sending node's application posts a send request (SendReq) while the receiver posts a receive request (RecvReq). Network interface cards (NIC) process this communication (Comm) in the background while the applications continue their computations. The applications later test the requests' terminations (SendEvent and RecvEvent)*

Message-passing may or may not be carried out after a *rendezvous*, i.e. a synchronization operation that enables the sender to find out whether the receiver is ready to receive. In this way, synchronizations and data transfers can be combined in a single communication. This operation necessitates a round-trip between the two machines to synchronize them. It therefore has a significant latency cost. From a positive point of view, the *rendezvous* prevents the receiver from having to copy unexpected data in an intermediate memory area. A balance is needed between the *rendezvous*'s additional latency (which is to be avoided in order to benefit from the low latency of small messages) and the additional cost of a memory copy if the receiver was not ready (to be avoided if the message is large). The decision is left to the application by the MPI interface, depending on whether it wishes the communications to be synchronous or not, and is sometimes also left to the MPI implementation itself, depending on network priorities.

4.2.5.2. *Case 2: remote access model*

In the second model, the communication primitives are remote-memory reading or writing, i.e. RDMA. The application defines windows (RDMA windows) in advance, the identifiers of which it gives to the other nodes. These nodes can then read and write remotely in the memory areas described by these windows. Here too, the more hardware resources and evolved functionalities offered by the card, the more the protocol can be offloaded there, and the more the overlap in the host will be improved.

In the message-passing model, two nodes are involved to establish the communication: data transfer is cooperative. Both nodes must submit a request and each is notified of its termination, see Figure 4.3; it is a two-sided communication. No change in the receiving process's address space is possible without its explicit participation. On the other hand, during an RDMA the target application has nothing to do (apart from creating the RDMA window in advance). It is therefore not notified of the termination of the communication; see Figure 4.4; it is a one-sided communication.

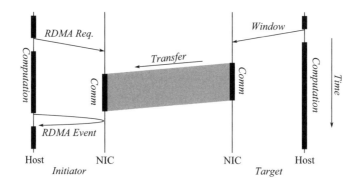

Figure 4.4. *Time diagram of a remote-memory read by RDMA. The application on the target node creates an RDMA window while the initiator posts a request (RDMAReq). Network interface cards (NIC) process this communication (Comm) in the background while the applications continue their computations. The initiating application later tests the request's termination (RDMAEvent)*

It must be noted that the notion of *rendezvous* does not exist for RDMA because the target node is not involved and has necessarily prepared the window in advance. One-sided communications therefore decouple the data transfers and the synchronization operations. These characteristics are summed up in Table 4.1.

Type of communication	Class	Initiator operation	Target	Rendezvous	Data
Message-passing	*Two-sided*	*Send*	*Recv*	Possible	to target
RDMA *Put*	*One-sided*	*Put*		No	to target
RDMA *Get*	*One-sided*	*Get*		No	to initiator

Table 4.1. *Summary of the characteristics of data transfer by message-passing or RDMA. Notification of an operation is only sent to the node that submits it*

Whereas it is quite easy to set up remote memory accesses on a message-passing-type programming interface, the contrary, i.e. integrating a message-passing interface on a remote-memory access mechanism, can be difficult. Indeed, the absence of notification on the target node forces polling to be used, which consumes processing time, particularly if it is necessary to wait for different messages being sent from different sources simultaneously. Furthermore, as several messages can be placed in the same RDMA window without the target application needing to reset this window, the different senders must be synchronized or use independent target windows. The popularity of MPI has forced extensive work so that it can be efficiently implemented on RDMA-based programming interfaces.

4.3. Description of the main high-performance networks

Here we present the main network technologies that have dominated the domain of computer clusters for about 15 years. We will follow them in chronological order and present Scalable Coherent Interface (SCI) first, then Myricom and Quadrics, before ending with the InfiniBand standard, which is much more recent.

4.3.1. *Dolphins SCI*

The SCI [GUS 92] technology was introduced at the beginning of the 1990s by Dolphin[1].

Its aim is to provide a very-low-latency, shared-memory mechanism. To do this, the interface cards develop a *bridge* between the memory bus of a machine and those of the remote nodes over the network.

The SCI network can be used by the SISCI (Software Interface for SCI) programming interface. It offers two main methods of communication by remote memory access. The first one consists of projecting remote memory segments in the local virtual memory (*shared memory*). Access to this projected memory produces rerouting through the interface card in a way that is transparent to the application. This enables a distributed shared memory to be very easily set up. The

---

1. Dolphin Interconnect Solutions, www.dolphinics.com.

second method consists of explicitly requesting remote memory access by primitives of the RDMA type.

These innovations have enabled SCI to be used in many works in the field of clusters. Recent models offer remote-memory-access latency of 1.4 μs, while bandwidth theoretically reaches 340 MB/s. Despite these positive factors, this technology does have certain limits:

– First, the network topology is a two-dimensional or three-dimensional ring or torus. The bandwidth sharing implied by this limits the actual throughput experienced by the applications. It also limits the possibility to increase the scale to large clusters.

– Second, communication processing is predominantly carried out by the host's processor, which considerably reduces the capacity for communication overlap.

– Finally, the shared memory-oriented programming model makes it difficult for the model to be used in large parallel applications because the message-passing model is very different. In fact, the implementation of the MPI interface on top of SISCI causes the latency experienced by the application to jump from about 1.5 to 4.5 μs. In addition to this, the amount of memory that can be projected into the remote memory is very limited. This makes it difficult for the shared memory-oriented model to be used on real applications, where resource needs are often great.

These different limits have led SCI technology to gradually disappear from the high-performance-computing market.

4.3.2. *Myricom Myrinet and Myri-10G*

Myricom[2] has long been the market leader in interconnection networks for computing clusters. The Myrinet network [BOD 95] appeared in 1995 and was involved very early on in the development of the specificities of fast networks, which we have listed in the previous section. Its main characteristics are that it is a technology designed

---

2. Myricom, Inc., www.myri.com.

to meet the needs of the MPI interface and high-performance and easy-to-program cards.

Myrinet technology has quickly become known for its excellent ability to scale to large clusters, thanks in part to its software drivers being designed for this context and in part to its network topology. Myrinet networks are organized in *clos* networks using switches that can assemble up to 512 links. The protocol uses source routing, which enables fast packet-transfer on the physical network, while reliability is ensured by checksum verification in the hardware. These characteristics have, for example, allowed the establishment of the *MareNostrum* cluster composed of 2,560 nodes in Barcelona. Supercomputing The flexible and programmable technology still remains a favored ground for experiments on routing strategies in clusters [GEO 08].

The interface cards embed a reduced instruction set computer (RISC) processor, the LANai, the latest versions of which run at more than 300 MHz. It has its own very fast (accessible in a few cycles) static RAM memory (generally 2 MB) and a powerful direct memory access engine. The open specifications of this hardware, the power of LANai and these cards' ease of reprogramming have led many to academic works on network protocols being carried out on Myrinet. Examples of such network protocol works include, for example, in Virtual Memory-Mapped Communication (VMMC) [DUB 97] and FastMessages (FM) [LAU 98].

Among the most interesting works, we must mention Basic Interface for Parallelism or BIP [PRY 97], which was developed in Lyon, France, and has long been the reference for the effective use of Myrinet networks. Its independent optimizations of small (using PIO and OS bypass) and large messages (using direct memory access and zero-copy) very early on has enabled a record latency of 3 μs to be reached and 96% of the links' capacity to be used. Use of the central processor is very low, which has enabled a very good overlap of communication by computing.

The official driver for Myrinet networks has long been GM (Group Message). Its interface is message-passing oriented. It is more robust than the academic software BIP but has inferior performance. Latency barely reaches $6\,\mu s$ on the most high-performance machines, at the price of rather significant processor consumption. The bandwidth observed with GM is good but this forces the application to explicitly record the memory areas involved in the communications. Furthermore, notification methods are very limited. Waiting for the termination of a particular request is impossible. This necessitates the use of a thread receiving network events in a single queue and the thread concerned to be woken up by the event received.

The average performances of GM, particularly compared to BIP, has led Myricom to develop a new driver called MX (Myrinet Express). The primary objective of MX is to provide performances similar to BIP with the robustness of GM and a more flexible programming interface. With most of the applications running on clusters with MPI applications, MX actually offers an interface that is very similar to MPI[3], based on the submission of non-blocking requests. Send and receive requests are associated by a flexible method of comparison of their parameters (matching). These advantages have led to its very fast deployment on most modern Myrinet clusters. Its latency today approaches $2\,\mu s$, while it easily saturates the physical links.

The third generation of Myricom hardware, Myri-10G, appeared in 2005. It enables MX to reach 10 Gbit/s by keeping the same latency. MX is now capable of supporting several links per card or aggregating several cards from the same machine. For example, it allows Tokyo's T2K Open Supercomputer reach 40 Gbit/s.

Besides this, Myricom has introduced convergence between fast cluster networks and traditional Ethernet networks. Like most fast-network software stacks, GM and MX have long offered the

---

3. Myrinet Express (MX): is a high-performance, low-level, message-passing interface for Myrinet. For further details, see www.myri.com/scs/MX/doc/mx.pdf.

encapsulation of traditional TCP/IP traffic in Myrinet packets in order to allow traditional applications to benefit to some extent from the fast network. This advantage of Myrinet technologies is that they have enabled us to physically connect Ethernet and Myrinet networks, ensuring, at the switch level, the translation of Ethernet packets encapsulated in GM or MX into native Ethernet frames.

This convergence reached its apex with Myri-10G cards, since Myrinet 10 G's physical cables are now the same as that of 10 G Ethernet. Myri-10G cards are therefore capable of speaking native MX or Ethernet, depending on the driver used by the OS. Only the packet-routing headers are different. This has naturally enabled the development of an MX solution transported on a traditional Ethernet network (MX-over-Ethernet or MXoE). With high-performance Ethernet switches (low latency between ports and high-performance flow control), this solution enables the implementation of high-performance message passing on small Ethernet networks as well as on native Myricom networks.

Next, the addition of translation functionalities between MX and Ethernet routing headers in switches allowed the creation of a transparent network mixing Ethernet and Myri-10G hosts as well as traditional MX and TCP/IP protocols. This, for example, enables specific machines such as BLUEGENE/P to access storage servers benefiting from MX performances without having to use MX themselves.

It is now possible to use the MX protocol on non-Myricom standard hardware, thanks to the software stack OPEN-MX [GOG 08a].

Traditional TCP/IP protocols can therefore be mixed with the MX protocol optimized for MPI regardless of whether the machine is equipped with standard Ethernet or Myri-10G hardware. Thanks to this concrete convergence, Myricom has succeeded in extending its market to that of standard Ethernet hardware in the world of storage and servers.

4.3.3. *Quadrics QsNet*

Quadrics[4] QsNet networks have long considered the Rolls Royce of fast networks, with exorbitant prices but unparalleled performance of close to $1\,\mu$s of latency and 900 MB/s of bandwidth. To achieve this, QsNet technology relies on very high-performance hardware and a few interesting software innovations.

The network is composed of switches forming a clos topology. The interface cards (called ELAN) are also very powerful and feature advanced functionalities. Unlike Myrinet, however, little research has been carried out on this material, mainly because its specifications are not open.

One of the particularities of ELAN cards is that they have an embedded Memory Management Unit (MMU), like machine processors. This circuit is capable of translating the virtual addresses passed by the application into physical addresses. It is a significant advantage where competitors must emulate MMU software to carry out this translation. This technological innovation is assisted by a modification in the OS that keeps the card's MMU constantly updated with the host's MMU. Therefore, zero-copy communications become very easy. It is through such innovations, along with the power of the hardware, that have enabled a very low latency and very high bandwidth to be achieved [PET 03].

QsNet networks are driven by the Elanlib programming interface, which is of the remote-memory-access type. To address applications of the MPI type, Quadrics has also supplied a dedicated interface called TPORTS (tagged message ports).

Quadrics had announced its intention to move towards convergence between Ethernet and fast networks, especially with "QsTenG" Ethernet switches, which were also expected to be capable of communicating with the future QsNet3 interfaces. However, with the former QsNet2

---

4. Quadrics, www.quadrics.com

technology being largely surpassed by Myri-10G or InfiniBand, and a large delay having been accumulated during QsNet3's development, Quadrics had to shut down in mid-2009.

4.3.4. *InfiniBand*

InfiniBand is a standard created at the end of the 1990s by a consortium of computer hardware manufacturers in order to define the architecture of future I/O operations. The initial idea was to define a standard input-output bus to replace the PCI bus as well storage and network[5] access systems. Finally, after some manufacturers dropped out – including Intel who announced that it had created PCI Express to replace the PCI bus – research was re-focused on high-performance networks [PFI 01]. This research has mainly been related to communications in computing clusters, but has also covered access storage devices, particularly Fiber Channel.

The processors of InfiniBand interface cards are now usually produced by Mellanox. The very attractive standard led to re-purchasing of most of the initial start-ups by large companies, which has led the current market to be dominated by Mellanox, Voltaire, Qlogic and Cisco.

The standard's specifications detail both hardware and software implementation. Each retailer can distribute its own software network-access software layers that more or less respect the norm.

The OpenIB[6] project has offered a free alternative to those produced by various proprietary software distributors. It is now distributed by the OpenFabrics[7] alliance, which became the official support body for InfiniBand networks and the technologies revolving around it, such as iWarp.

---

5. Details of the architecture specifications for InfiniBand Trade Association can be found at www.infinibandta.org.

6. OpenIB Alliance, www.openib.org.

7. Open Fabrics Alliance, www.openfabrics.org.

The design of the InfiniBand network is actually looking increasingly like a high-performance Ethernet network rather than a network that is fundamentally designed for computing clusters. It is intrinsically incompatible with Ethernet, which limits its adoption in markets outside scientific computing. Its low-level protocol is, however, similar to Ethernet. The topology is not fixed and routing is carried out in switches. The network can therefore be organized in a *clos network* or in simpler topologies, depending on the needs.

The main interface is the Verbs Application Programming Interface (VAPI) which resembles VIA (Virtual Interface Architecture). Low-level communications benefit from the hardware's RDMA capacities to get very good performance. Parallel applications continue to use MPI on InfiniBand, either through the OpenMPI project [GAB 04] that is backed by many manufacturers and supports a wide range of hardware, or by the specific implementation of MVAPICH[8] within which a great deal of experimental research on InfiniBand is carried out.

The theoretical bandwidth is currently 1.6 GB/s using interface cards with two InfiniBand $4\times$ double data rate[9] links. Despite this, the limits of the I/O buses of the machines still make such performances difficult to achieve. The generalization of PCI Express should solve this problem, but the announcement of Quad Data Rate cards should re-open the gap between theoretical and observed performance.

The latency obtained on InfiniBand, which is between 5 and $10\,\mu s$, has long been a big problem for the generalization of the standard because other high-performance networks have easily reduced their latency to less than $3\,\mu s$. In practice, the implementation is entirely based on RDMA, which poses scalability problems, but has also strongly impacted latency. The standard and implementation have

---

8. MVAPICH stands for MPI for InfiniBand over VAPI Layer and is based in the Network-Based Computing Lab at the Ohio State University. Details about the VAPI Layer can be found at nowlab.cse.ohio-state.edu/projects/mpi-iba/.

9. $4 \times 250\,\mathrm{MB/s} \times \times 2$ (double data rate) $\times \times 0.8$ (encoding $8/10$) $= 1.6\,\mathrm{GB/s}$.

recently been reviewed to fix this problem. The use of PIO instead of RDMA for small messages now enables Mellanox's Connectx cards to approach 1 μs of latency.

The scalability problem was due in part to the high memory consumption of connections and in part to the necessity to poll a specific resource at each connection when a message is expected on a specific connection. Indeed, as for SISCI, the absence of notification on the RDMA's target machine forces it to use polling. In addition to consuming processing time, this strategy is not scalable when the number of messages or nodes increases. The recent introduction of the Shared Receive Queue (SRQ) concept has enabled the factorization of these needs and therefore the reduction of their cost in very large clusters. This is, in fact, a disguised dropping of the all-RDMA concept (which was originally InfiniBand's slogan) to give way to a strategy similar to message-passing, which has made the Myrinet and QsNet networks successful in the past.

4.3.5. *Synthesis of the characteristics of high-performance networks*

Table 4.2 summarizes the main characteristics of the different high-performance networks used in computing clusters. Cluster networks obtain higher performances than Ethernet by using dedicated programming interfaces and advanced functionalities in the card.

To this day, the InfiniBand technology has a significant lead in terms of performance, achieving close to 3 GB/s in bandwidth and 1 μs in latency. This is reflected by the use of InfiniBand in 30% of the biggest computers (Top500 [SIT 09], classification of the most powerful machines in the world). In addition to its opening the traditional Ethernet technologies market, Myri-10G is the technology that is best equipped to challenge InfiniBand. This is thanks, in particular, to a model that is perfectly adapted to message-passing, where InfiniBand continues to suffer from its RDMA model. The difference in performance is such, however, that applications that prefer Myricom technologies are increasingly rare.

Technology (protocol)	Ethernet10G (IP)	SCI (SISCI)	Myri-10G (MX)	QsNet (Elanlib)	InfiniBand (Verbs)
Interface	Socket	RDMA	messages	RDMA + notification	RDMA + SRQ
Zero-copy	no	no	except small messages	except small messages	except small messages
Registration	no	yes	yes	no if system modified	Yes
CPU use	large (copy)	large (PIO copy)	low (DMA)	low (DMA)	low (DMA)
Topology	Variable	ring or torus	Clos	Clos	Clos or variable
Theoretical bandwidth (MB/s)	$\simeq 1,250$ +1,250	340 shared	1,250 +1,250	900 +900	1,500 +1,500
Latency (μs)	$\simeq$ 15–50	1–3	2 3	1–?	1–5
Ethernet and IP compatibility	Yes Yes	No No	Yes Yes	Soon? Yes	No Yes

Table 4.2. *Comparison of high-performance networks in terms of programming interface, zero-copy communications, need to prepare memory-areas involved (registering), use of the central processor to process communications, topology, raw performances, and compatibility with IP and Ethernet*

4.4. Convergence between fast and traditional networks

The hegemony of fast networks in the domain of computing clusters is increasingly contested. In the past 12 years, clusters have emerged that use traditional networks – Fast Ethernet, Gigabit Ethernet and more recently 10-Gigabit Ethernet – and occupy more than half of the Top500. This is partly due to the transfer of technological advances from the fast networks to the regular ones. Indeed, innovations such as DMA, which used to be the brand image of Myrinet and the like, are now used by every Ethernet card to reduce the central processor's load.

A great deal of research has been carried out to improve the performance of protocol layers with help from the hardware. Programmable cards have been proposed, as well as advanced functionalities such as TCP Offload Engine (TOE), which relieves the host from network management. However, these complex technologies were not easily adopted. Now, the cards are used for simpler operations that do not need to be synchronized with the host (stateless offload). This is the case of transmit segmentation offload (TSO) and large receive offload (LRO), which considerably reduce the number of packets needed to be processed in the host by using the card to cut them up into Ethernet frames and then re-assemble them. These strategies mean that now 10G-Ethernet cards are prevented from saturating the central processor of the machine, without the necessity for intrusive modification of the software layers.

Even if the performance for throughput and processor consumption is very good, however, they remain quite a long way from fast networks, especially in terms of latency. As is often the case, the TCP/IP software stack, with its interface ill-adapted to parallel applications, is considered responsible. Many works are emerging with the aim of implementing a software stack based on Ethernet adapted to computing clusters.

In fact, Ethernet is increasingly appearing to be an interesting transport layer for local networks and clusters. The AOE[10] protocol was a precursor in the domain. It offered storage sharing directly over the Ethernet. Today, the popularization of FCOE[11] has confirmed this tendency. Beyond storage, the question of MPI-like communications over Ethernet is posed.

Research started about 15 years ago on efficient Ethernet exploitation for MPI communications. For example, the GAMMA project [CIA 00] suggested modifying Ethernet drivers. Latency can reach $6\,\mu s$, which is very interesting, taking into consideration the price of the hardware used. The necessity to modify drivers at the expense of traditional TCP/IP communication, however, severely hinders the expansion of this idea.

---

10. ATA-over-Ethernet, www.coraid.com.
11. Fiber Channel over Ethernet, www.fcoe.com.

A more standardized approach was proposed with iWarp, which has now been integrated with OpenIB by the Open Fabrics Alliance. iWarp suggested an RDMA-type interface over Ethernet, similar to the interface based on the fast network technologies that InfiniBand proposes. iWarp was designed for advanced Ethernet cards (RDMA-enabled NIC), which are capable of processing remote memory access in Internet protocol-type connections. This enables memory copies to be suppressed, thus avoiding the cost of the usual TCP/IP protocol layers.

This model allows interesting performances [RAS 07], but they are limited to these special Ethernet cards. The hardware being rather uncommon and expensive, it is hard to justify choosing it over a fast network with better performance. In the case of long-distance communication where fast networks cannot be used, however, the iWarp idea is somewhat interesting.

The convergence between Ethernet and Myrinet networks (see section 4.3.2) proposed by Myricom already allows the execution of MPI applications with a very low latency ($2\,\mu$s) and a high speed on a standard 10 Gbit/s Ethernet network. It requires Myri-10G interface cards to function in native MX mode and not just any standard Ethernet interface, which limits its dissemination and that of iWarp. Works on OPEN-MX crossed this gap by offering software implementation of MX on any Ethernet hardware interface. By combining this implementation with the advanced functionalities of modern I/O controllers, such as the offloading of memory copies[12], it is possible to get very good performance [GOG 08b] without making modified cards mandatory, in the way that iWarp does.

It therefore appears to be increasingly clear that Ethernet networks will be part of the future of scientific computing and parallel applications. Many works have been proposed in order to improve

---

12. Intel I/O Acceleration Technology, http://www.intel.com/network/connectivity/vtc_ioat.htm.

performance and integrate them with fast networks. The form this convergence will take remains to be seen.

4.5. Conclusion

Table 4.3 presents a summary of the principles mentioned in this chapter.

Principle	Type	Other context of exploitation
Zero-copy communications	software	Yes
OS bypass	software	Multimedia applications-ALF
Interrupt management	software	1 or 10 Gbit/s high speed Ethernet
Offload of processing to the card (NIC)	software	1 or 10 Gbit/s high speed Ethernet
Increase of network reliability	hardware	Wide-area optical networks
Source routing	software, hardware	?

Table 4.3. *Summary of the principles implemented in high-performance cluster networks to reduce latency*

Chapter 5

The Challenge of Throughput and Distance

5.1. Obstacles to high rate

In Chapter 1, we saw that the grid paradigm had been introduced to respond to significant needs in terms of computing, as well as in terms of processing and storage of large quantities of information, such as in CERN's *Large Hadron Collider Computing Grid*[1] project.

Beyond this symbolic example, other domains have identified the grid as the ideal tool for processing their very large databases. In the medical domain, the grid paradigm is explored for very large-scale applications, such as epidemiology, statistical analysis of large populations, medical simulation or research on rare diseases. For example, the annual image production of a radiology department exceeds 10 terabytes. Similarly, in the domain of genomics, the flood of biological data produced by very large-scale experiments will be one of the greatest challenges of the next few years. These applications need to transfer significant amounts of data, not only from their acquisition point to computing centers for processing, but also to move them

---

1. http://lcg.web.cern.ch/LCG/.

between the storage spaces, store them and make them available to large and very wide-spread communities.

In [SAN 05], the need for high throughput to carry out these massive data transfers was identified as the main challenge for grid networks. In this document, the OGF (Open Grid Forum) alerts grid users about the limits of the common protocols and their software. It shows, in particular, the difficulties related to the use of the Transport Control Protocol or TCP in grid contexts. As for [VIC 05b], it summarizes the variations of TCP that are proposed for very high-speed networks.

In this chapter, we analyze this specific issue and detail the principles, mechanisms and alternatives used today by programmers and users of intensive, distributed computing and storage infrastructures. We note that this problem of high-speed massive transfers in a long-distance context is shared by content delivery networks, and that some solutions advocated here can therefore be adapted to it and vice versa.

Obtaining high throughput in a computing grid is a complex problem, in part because of the heterogeneous nature of the underlying network interconnection, and in part due to the intrinsic inadequacy of the TCP protocol, designed for fair bandwidth sharing and not for the individual performance of streams. Highlighting its inadequacy to long distances has increased the amount of research on congestion control using an anticipation mechanism based on sliding windows, as well as the amount of high-speed TCP variants. Today it is difficult for grid-application users or programmers to know which solution to adopt to benefit the most from their infrastructure.

Below, we list the main obstacles preventing users from obtaining a high throughput:
    – congestion on one of the two end systems (sender or receiver);
    – badly-configured protocol;
    – inefficient and unadapted protocol;
    – blocking operations;
    – application programming interface limitations.

The main paths possible for getting around them, which are presented in the rest of this chapter, are:

– adjustment of the configuration parameters;

– use of parallel connections;

– increase in size of the packets transmitted;

– explicit congestion notification;

– protocol modification;

– reuse of the techniques for high-performance cluster networks;

– use of the techniques for overlay networks;

– setup of dedicated optical paths.

In the following sections, these different alternatives are discussed. They are illustrated in Chapter 10. Prior to this, we review the characteristics of TCP, which is the most frequently used protocol for transferring data in a grid. We highlight the design choices, in particular the congestion-control mechanism, that prevent individual connection from reaching a high average throughput.

5.2. Operating principle and limits of TCP congestion control

One of TCP's most important and critical mechanisms is the congestion-control mechanism defined to ensure fair bandwidth sharing between all users of a network. This mechanism was introduced at the end of the 1980s, following persistent anomalies where the throughput of applications ended up being abnormally reduced. This phenomenon was caused by an influx of users that was too great for the network capacities (causing congestion) and by bad handling of the retransmission of packets lost due to that congestion.

Anticipated by John Nagle [NAG 84] as early as 1984, this type of anomaly is commonly called *congestion collapse*. In the years 1986–1988, the effective throughput of the link joining the Lawrence Berkeley Laboratory (LBL) to the University of California, Berkeley, although less than 400 m long, regularly went from 32 kbit/s to 40 bit/s, a throughput reduction by a factor of 1,000.

To counter these performance problems, Van Jacobson of the LBL, suggested in 1988 [JAC 88] introducing a series of distributed algorithms in the TCP protocol to be in charge of controlling network congestion. The main idea was to propose a robust mechanism capable of quickly and effectively detecting signs of congestion. Since, by design, an Internet Protocol (IP) network does not give off any explicit signal indicating the congestion status, the detection of packet loss is interpreted as a saturation of the capacity of the network equipment crossed by the TCP connection. Losses are detected based on a timer's expiration (RTO (Retransmission Timeout)) calculated using the round trip time (RTT) or the reception of acknowledgements for duplicated packets.

The first mechanism introduced consists in forcing every new connection to gradually increase its throughput according to the Slow Start algorithm, to prevent its network path from becoming saturated too quickly.

5.2.1. *Slow Start*

In this phase, the sending process seeks to estimate the maximum quantity of packets it can transmit before causing a loss in the network. The quantity of packets transmissible (called a congestion window) at a given moment is internally represented by the variable *cwnd*. *Cwnd* is incremented each time a packet acquittal is received:

$$ACK: \quad cwnd \longleftarrow cwnd + 1 \qquad [5.1]$$

In spite of its name, it is a rather aggressive phase because the number of packets sent doubles every RTT. The left part of Figure 5.1 illustrates the evolution of the congestion window's size during the Slow Start phase. However, this exponential increase is limited by the

Slow Start threshold (*ssthreshold*), beyond which the evolution of the congestion window's size enters the congestion avoidance phase.

In the case of packet-loss before this threshold is crossed, the congestion window and the *ssthreshold* are divided by two and the algorithm moves on to the next phase. A loss too early in the Slow Start phase can severely penalize a stream because it will start the next phase much further from the maximum network capacity. It also has consequences in the long term because the output threshold is reduced.

5.2.2. *Congestion avoidance*

This phase consists of slowly increasing the size of the congestion window to try to send as much as possible, and quickly decreasing the window size in the case of packet-loss, as a conservative measure. For this, an algorithm called Additive Increase Multiplicative Decrease (AIMD) is used. Its stability and convergence properties were proven by Jain in 1989 [CHI 89]:

$$ACK: \quad cwnd \longleftarrow cwnd + \frac{\alpha}{cwnd} \qquad [5.2]$$

With delayed acknowledgements or accurate byte counting (ABC – counting the congestion window in bytes rather than in packets), we end up with a congestion-window increase of 1 per RTT, as illustrated on the right of Figure 5.1.

In case of packet loss due to the timer's expiration (RTO), the algorithm returns to the Slow Start phase.

5.2.3. *Fast Retransmit*

To avoid false detection of the expiration of a packet's timer, the timer value used – the RTO – must be very large compared to the RTT (typically around four times bigger than the RTT with a minimum value of 200 ms). The drawback is then that it is necessary to wait for,

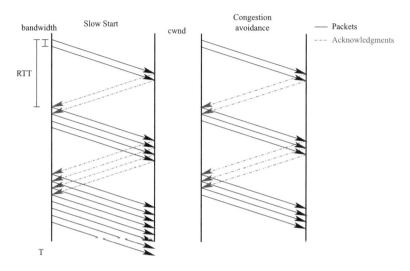

Figure 5.1. *Evolution of the size of the congestion window in the Slow Start and congestion avoidance phases*

potentially, a very long time before being able to retransmit and send new packets. This can dramatically reduce the send rate. To overcome this problem, the mechanism called Fast Retransmit is used if three duplicate acknowledgements matching the same sequence number are received. The packet just after this sequence number is then considered to have been lost and is immediately retransmitted. The TCP variant that uses this Fast Retransmit mechanism is TCP NewReno.

$$Loss: \quad cwnd \longleftarrow cwnd - \beta * cwnd \qquad [5.3]$$

In Van Jacobson's proposition, the value of the constants used for the increment α is 1 and decrement β is $\frac{1}{2}$. Disregarding implementation subtleties, delayed acknowledgements or ABC, we end up with a congestion-window increase of 1 per RTT, as illustrated on the right of Figure 5.1.

In the case of packet loss due to the timer's expiration (RTO), the algorithm returns to the Slow Start phase.

Figure 5.2 gives an idea of the evolution of the size of the congestion window over time when these two algorithms are used. W designates the maximum size of the congestion window that the connection can achieve.

Later on, many improvements were suggested to improve congestion control in specific cases (SACK (Selective Acknowledgment) for detecting multiple losses, for example). For 20 years now, all the implementations of the TCP stack have been based on these principles.

The current reference version of TCP is called TCPReno (or NewReno, which optimizes the retransmission mechanism as described above). In the rest of this chapter, the term TCP refers to TCP NewReno.

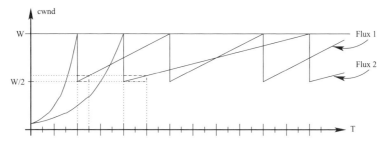

Figure 5.2. *Evolution of the congestion window for two TCP connections with an RTT value of t and 2t, respectively*

5.2.4. *Analytical model*

Models were proposed to analyze TCP's performance depending on characteristic network parameters. The most well-known is the one suggested by Padhye in 1998 [PAD 98a], which defines a TCP response function (the achievable throughput) that depends on the loss rate (p), the RTT, the value of the RTO timer and the maximum size of TCP segments (maximum segment size or MSS):

$$R = \frac{MSS}{RTT * \sqrt{\frac{2p}{3}} + RTO * \min(1, 3\sqrt{3p/8}) * p(1 + 32p^2)} \quad [5.4]$$

The simplified model proposed by Mathis [MAT 97] is often used:

$$R = \frac{MSS}{RTT} * \frac{C}{p^d} \qquad\qquad [5.5]$$

It does not take into consideration certain aspects of congestion control, such as the packet-retransmission mechanism. It has the advantage of being simple. C, the coefficient of proportionality, is a constant that integrates aspects related to the implementation of congestion control (i.e. AIMD constants), acknowledgement management (i.e. whether sending is delayed or not on the receiver) or loss distribution in the network (i.e. random losses or losses solely on congestion). d represents the cost of the protocol's response in the face of a given loss rate over throughput.

In the case of TCP, with losses on congestion only and no delayed-acknowledgement, C is $\sqrt{\frac{3}{2}}$ and d is $\frac{1}{2}$.

This model is compatible with Padhye's in the case of a low loss rate (which is often the case in modern wired networks). It is valid when assuming to be in a permanent regime with data to transmit continuously (massive data transfers, not short-duration ones) and that the RTT is constant (absence of congestion and/or state variations of the routers' waiting queues).

Figure 5.2 also illustrates the impact of the RTT on TCP. Indeed, the TCP feedback loop is based on the RTT: the progression of the congestion window is limited by the return time of the acknowledgements. If the RTT doubles, the congestion window's growth speed is divided by two. This is problematic when the RTT is very high.

5.3. Limits of TCP over long distances

This section presents a few of the limitations of TCP over long distances.

The model presented in section 5.2.4 highlights the impact of the value of RTT on performance. At constant rate, to compensate for an RTT multiplied by 10, the loss-rate would need to be divided by 100 to keep the same throughput. Thus, to obtain a continuous 10 Gbit/s transfer on a link with 100 ms of RTT using 1,500-byte packets, only one loss every 5E9 packets should occur, at worst, which is difficult to guarantee even on optical networks.

Table 5.1 [FLO 03] presents the highest possible loss rates acceptable in order to achieve a given average throughput.

In addition to this, if the buffer memory is not large enough (for example if the edge router is not correctly dimensioned) the protocol will only be able to operate at 75% of its capacity, on average. This is problematic at 10 Gbit/s, because 25% of 10 Gbit/s corresponds to a very significant throughput loss. Another limit of the protocol is the fact that it is impossible to distinguish losses due to congestion from losses due to a bad-quality link, which is typically the case for wireless networks. The protocol therefore cannot operate optimally when this type of network is present in the grid interconnection.

TCP throughput (Mbit/s)	Delay between two losses	*cwnd* max	p max
1	5.5	8.3	0.02
10	55.5	83.3	0.0002
100	555.5	833.3	0.000002
1,000	5555.5	8333.3	0.00000002
10,000	55555.5	83333.3	0.0000000002

Table 5.1. *Delay (in number of RTTs) between two loss events for TCP with 1,500-byte packets and an RTT of 100 ms, maximum size of congestion window (in number of segments) and loss rates*

It is also noteworthy that the receiver can explicitly limit the size of the sender's congestion window by using the *advertised window* field in the acknowledgements it returns. This option is typically used if the receiver considers itself to be incapable of processing all the packets at the speed imposed by the sender (flow-control mechanism). This can be a major cause of performance loss.

Also worth noting is that TCP is not a good protocol for flows operating with different RTTs. The flows with the lowest RTTs will be favored because they are capable of receiving acknowledgements from their receiver much faster, and therefore they are capable of increasing the rate they use at greater speed, to the detriment of flows with longer RTTs.

The format of TCP headers was not designed for such a significant increase in the order of magnitude of network rates. For this reason, in the TCP specification the maximum size of the usable window was initially 64 kB. An option, called *window scale* was added to allow this to be multiplied by a power of two. Window sizes going up to 1 GB can now be used: TCP could therefore theoretically still be functional on 100 Gbit/s links if the RTT is less than 80 ms.

5.4. Configuration of TCP for high speed

The machines connected to the grid often have high-speed interfaces (typically 1 Gbit/s). As we saw in Chapter 4, different hardware configuration problems can prevent a high speed being obtained compared to the theoretical speed of the interface card. In the case of the massive transfers considered here, exchanges are carried out between the discs of two remote systems and no longer between two application processes, as in the case of interprocess communications.

Furthermore, the TCP protocol requires a specific configuration for the high-speed and long-latency context, to allow the default values of the operating system to be changed – these are often configured for the traditional Internet. All this constitutes what is commonly called the *wizard gap* [MAT 03] and is a true headache for grid programmers and users. Indeed, the latter must know their hardware and software architecture perfectly in order to be able to optimize the system's configuration and obtain the desired performances. This is the reason that we detail the main factors of configuration to be considered as well as the nominal values to choose below.

5.4.1. *Hardware configurations*

Figure 5.3 is a synthetic presentation of the different steps necessary for sending data from disk to disk on a network:

(1) data copy from disk to RAM via the PCI (Peripheral Component Interconnect) bus;

(2) data routing to the processor for processing (splitting up into packets);

(3) packet copy in RAM in the transmission queue;

(4) packet copy in the card via the PCI bus;

(5) packet routing on the network after waiting in a queue;

(6) packet processing in a router after waiting in a queue.

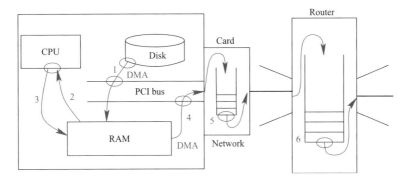

Figure 5.3. *Different bottlenecks in traditional hardware architectures*

Receiver-side similar (symmetrical) operations are carried out to route packets from the network card to the disk. The ellipses indicate the places where potential hardware bottlenecks exist: input/output on disks, the PCI bus, the CPU, the RAM and the buffer memory. These potential bottlenecks are sometimes difficult to locate. The user will therefore need to use an automatic detection tool, such as the PATHNIF tool created by the French National Institute for Research in Computer Science and Control (INRIA).

5.4.2. *Software configuration*

To succeed in maintaining the maximum speed, it is necessary to use a buffer (TCP socket buffer) with a size greater than or equal to the bandwidth-delay product. One of the main problems with this approach is that it significantly increases latency on the path, which can have inconveniences for applications that are very latency-sensitive (voice applications). In the default configuration of many operating systems, the value is too low to achieve good performances (for example 64 kB for the GNU/Linux kernel). It is this last parameter that is typically the source of 95% of TCP configuration problems.

Figure 5.4 suggests the quantity of buffer memory necessary for emission. By adopting a fluid view of the network, the bandwidth-delay product (BDP) represents the quantity of data that must be transmitted in order to completely fill a pipe where the length is delay and the diameter is bandwidth. This represents the optimal use of the resource when the path experiences no congestion.

In the first scenario, the size of the congestion window is less than the BDP. It is necessary, with TCP, to wait until the acknowledgements matching the data have been received before continuing to transmit, so moments of silence are observed between two emissions of a packet group (TCP sends packets in bursts).

In the second scenario, the size of the congestion window is more than the BDP: a sufficient quantity of packets can be sent for the acknowledgements unblocking new packet emissions to arrive, at the latest, when the last packet is sent. If the size of the buffer memory used by the sender is equal to at least twice the BDP, it is possible to continually send at maximum speed if there is no congestion. If a packet is lost, even after dividing the congestion window, it is still possible to send a number of packets equal to BDP on the link, thereby completely filling it. However, this causes a significant increase in delay because of the time necessary to cross queues.

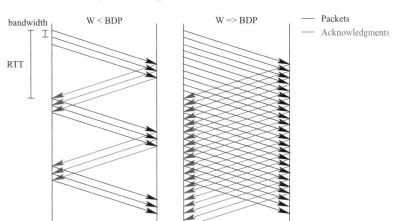

Figure 5.4. *Importance of the relative size of the congestion window and the bandwidth-delay product*

In the GNU/Linux kernel, four parameters are used to define buffer memory: *rmem_max* and *wmem_max* to determine, respectively, the maximum read and write size (in bytes) available for all open connections; *tcp_rmem* and *tcp_wmem* that are triplets of values (in bytes) corresponding to the minimum, initial and maximum memory value that the TCP sockets can occupy during read and write, respectively. It is therefore necessary to ensure that a minimum value equal to the BDP can be allocated so that the performance is not reduced.

Since 2001, a mechanism for the autoconfiguration of the size of the memory allocated to a TCP socket has been implemented in the kernel. It consists of increasing the size of the memory allocated to a socket when its needs increase, i.e. when the size of the congestion window increases. However, it is still necessary to make sure that the values provided in the parameters presented above allow a value of at least one BDP to be reached.

It is noteworthy that if *setsockopt()* (a function for updating the parameters of a socket) is called to update the size of TCP buffers, then the value provided is automatically doubled by the kernel if possible. The autoconfiguration mechanism is then deactivated.

5.4.3. *Parameters of network card drivers*

Interrupt Coalescence (IC) is a method that consists of waiting for a certain number of packets to be received before raising the interrupt that signals to the kernel that it can extract packets from the network card. The effect is therefore similar to an aggregation of these interrupts to limit the number of times the kernel is interrupted to get packets.

NAPI is the new application programming interface used by the GNU/Linux kernel to process packets, no longer one by one but all those that are available in a network card at the time the kernel comes to get packets. It is preferable to activate this functionality when a very high-speed network is used.

One parameter that should also be correctly positioned is *txqueuelen*. It corresponds to the maximum number of packets that can be placed in the queue before the network card. If this number is too small, in some cases the card cannot be fed packets quickly enough and performance decreases. Ten thousand is a good value for a 1 Gbit/s link with 100 ms of RTT. The point here is that every time the card looks for packets in the queue, it finds some; this is guaranteed if *txqueuelen* is of the same order of magnitude as the maximum size of the congestion window. This has a greater impact on the sender.

Table 5.2 sums up the parameters that need to be used to obtain an optimum value.

5.5. Alternative congestion-control approaches to that of standard TCP

This section presents a few large families of solutions that have been introduced over the past few years in order to correct TCP's

Name	Parametering	$C_a = 1\,\text{Gbit/s}$	$C_a = 10\,\text{Gbit/s}$
TCP buffer memory	$> C_a * RTT$	11.9 MB	119 MB
txqueuelen	$> W$	10,000	100,000
ndev_max_bklg	$ndev\_max\_bklg*$	350	3,500
	$HZ * \bar{s} > C_a$		

Table 5.2. *Summary table of software parameters for TCP and examples for 300 HZ and RTT = 100 ms*

performance problem. It should be noted that the problematic point is TCP's congestion control, which is not reactive enough in the context of long latencies. The other properties of TCP, such as reliable transport or fair bandwidth sharing, are more than desired and should become essential. These properties should be part of a solution that, in the long run, will replace TCP in any context.

5.5.1. *Use of parallel flows*

The first approach adopted by grid users to solve TCP's performance problems was to implement massive data transfers by multiplexing several parallel connections. The idea, as shown in Figure 5.5, is to interleave the different sawtooth waves of several TCP flows in order to maximize the quantity of data sent, and therefore the throughput.

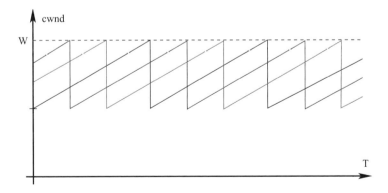

Figure 5.5. *Interleaving of several parallel flows*

In [ALT 06], Altman showed that it was possible to tend towards a theoretical throughput limit by increasing the number of parallel flows used. In practice, when reaching a certain number of flows, performance drops because of the software cost of using several processes and due to the limited space in the routers' buffers:

$$\bar{x}(N) = C * \left(1 - \frac{1}{1 + \frac{1+\beta}{1-\beta} * N} \right) \qquad [5.6]$$

In practice, this technique turns out to be relatively efficient and is very often adopted, directly in grid applications or via adapted file-transfer services. It is notably the technique used by the GridFTP software [ALL 03], from Globus middleware. GridFTP, defined as an extension of FTP that enables the use of parallel flows to carry out file transfers, was standardized by the OGF. The file to transfer is divided into several *chunks* whose emission is shared over several different flows, whether from several machines or a single one. It is up to the users to indicate the number of parallel flows they wish to use by providing a minimum and a maximum value; they must do the same for the buffer memory's size; which must be explicitly specified.

The biggest problem with this approach is succeeding to determine the ideal number of parallel flows required in order to get an optimum result, while trying to limit the impact on the other communications that find themselves faced with a traffic that is n times more aggressive than a normal TCP flow.

The well-known advantage of stream parallelization is that it compensates for performance problems without solving them, whether they are due to the hardware of end systems or to the configuration or type of protocol used. This approach is compatible with all the other improvements and alternatives presented below and can therefore be combined with them. The approach of transfer by stream parallelization was also used in "peer-to-peer" networks, and in particular in the BitTorrent software. Furthermore, it must be noted that this approach does not respect the principle of fair bandwidth sharing and must therefore be adopted cautiously in the Internet, and preferably only in dedicated networks.

5.5.2. *TCP modification*

The analysis in section 5.5.1 showed that in the case of long distances, TCP requires modifications to reduce the long latency of the feedback loop. The protocol has therefore been improved on several points.

5.5.2.1. *Slow Start modifications*

In theory and according to Padhye's formula, to achieve a window size W (typically BDP or 2 * BDP) at the end of the Slow Start phase, it is necessary to wait $log_2 W * RTT$ seconds. This phase can be very long if the RTT is significant, for example in the order of 100 ms, as is the case in a transfer between Europe and America. To solve this problem, different solutions were proposed. Some consider an even faster growth in the size of the congestion window (Limited Slow-Start, Fast Start [PAD 98b]), or even completely short-circuiting the Slow Start phase or try to get indications from intermediate equipment to quickly determine at what rate to start sending (Quick-Start [SAR 06]).

Slow Start's acceleration is important when the transfer ends before the Slow Start phase does. Its interest is more limited for massive data transfers in which Slow Start only represents a low percentage of the total transfer time. In the case of a transfer of 1 gigabyte on a network with a 1 Gbit/s rate and 100 ms RTT, the BDP is equal to about 12 MB. During the Slow Start phase, about 2W packets will be sent, which corresponds to a little more than 2% of the total transfer. This is negligible compared to the rest of the transfer. It is assumed that the only time Slow Start is used is in a massive data transfer.

It must be noted, however, that when an application stops communicating, even for a few fractions of a second, the connection returns into Slow Start mode. In the case of sporadic transfers of very large Message-Passing Interface messages, it is thus possible to end up in such a situation of frequent Slow Starts. In these applications, Slow Start modifications often turn out to be very useful.

5.5.2.2. *Methods of congestion detection*

5.5.2.2.1. Loss

The most traditional method for detecting congestion is detection by loss. Congestion is considered to exist from the moment it is noticed that a packet has been lost (explicit loss notification, timer expiry on waiting for acknowledgement, reception of duplicated acknowledgements, etc.).

It is used in TCP as well as in the majority of its variants for large-BDP networks such as, for example, HighSpeed-TCP [FLO 03], Hamilton-TCP [SHO 04] or CUBIC [RHE 05].

5.5.2.2.2. Delay

Another congestion indicator is the increase in the size of queues in the network. This is generally done by tracking the evolution of delay in the network. Congestion is detected when the delay exceeds a certain threshold relative to the delay expected on the network path.

TCP-Vegas [BRA 94] and FAST-TCP [WEI 06] are examples of TCP variants that use this method. Their implementations are rather unpopular because delay measurement lacks accuracy and cannot guarantee sufficient system stability.

5.5.2.2.3. Hybrid

A third category of congestion detection is a combination of the two previous ones. Generally, one of the types of indicators (typically detection by losses) serves as a primary congestion detector and its effect is moderated or accentuated by the other method (typically detection by delay).

TCP-Illinois [LIU 06] and TCP Compound [TAN 06] are examples of TCP variants using this model.

5.5.2.2.4. Assistance of network equipment

One last large category is that of TCP variations that use information provided by intermediate equipment (where losses due to congestion are known or are expected to occur). This is generally done by using one or several bit(s) from TCP headers to feed information back to the sender. It is used by many variations such as ECN [RAM 99] and XCP [KAT 02]. The main problem with this category is that it requires the use of specific hardware in routers, which poses a very significant deployment problem in a system on the scale of the Internet.

5.5.2.3. *Bandwidth-control methods*

5.5.2.3.1. Control by window size

This method is the one that is traditionally used by TCP. It consists of making packet sending dependent upon the existence of credits, created by a congestion window, that are consumed and regenerated[2] as packets are sent and acknowledgements received.

It is more difficult to foresee the throughput of a source from its congestion window when there are queues. This control mechanism contributes to the appearance of traffic bursts in the network because, except for the intervention of a packet-spacing mechanism, packets will be sent at the time when credits are renewed, i.e. upon acknowledgement reception.

5.5.2.3.2. Control by rate

This method consists of sending only a limited quantity of data during a given time interval. The rate at which a source is allowed to send is thus fixed. An additional mechanism can be added to make what can be sent vary over time in order to dynamically adapt to the evolution of network parameters.

One of the examples is TFRC [FLO 00] for TCP Friendly Rate Control. It uses the rate equation proposed by Padhye [PAD 98a] and

---

2. Even increased in algorithms used by TCP, see section 5.2.

an estimator of loss rates for determining the rate at which to send. It was designed to offer an equitable bandwidth when it occurs with TCP flows, but still maintains a bandwidth that is much less variable than with TCP. As a consequence, it is much less reactive to abrupt changes in bandwidth. This is also the case for the User Datagram Protocol (UDP) or DCCP (Datagram Congestion Control Protocol).

5.5.3. *UDP-based approaches*

Using another transport protocol can also be a solution to the problem of latency. UDP [POS 80] is a very simple transport protocol thatprovides only packet-sending and segment-integrity-control services. It is traditionally used in all applications for which TCP's retransmission on loss can strongly deteriorate performances. (In other words, it can be used for applications that rely heavily on inter-packet latency, such as voice-over-IP, video-on-demand, etc.).

These approaches nevertheless can necessitate the implementation of a reliability mechanism at the application level since UDP does not provide this service. It is therefore up to the application to control the sending rate in order to prevent the network from becoming too congested, thus reducing performance for all users. If the situation is favorable, for example a private link with few losses little concurrent traffic, UDP-based approaches enable continuous sending at a given rate and enable us to do without TCP's congestion-avoidance mechanism.

UDT (UDP-based Data Transfer) [GU 07] is an example of such a UDP-based variation. It is placed at the application level to manage a reliable end-to-end connection by using UDP as a transport protocol. It uses an explicit mechanism of acknowledgements and non-acknowledgements in order to manage reliability and retransmissions.

This protocol was developed to also enable a high modularity of the congestion control used at the application level. Therefore UDT is capable of emulating the behavior of any congestion-control method in order to adapt to the context of concurrent flows on the network.

Finally, even though UDP was developed for controlled environments where few flows occur at the same time, it is also possible to use it in a shared-network context such as the Internet because congestion control is supposed to be sufficiently adaptive to attenuate UDP's aggressiveness on the network.

5.6. Exploration of TCP variants for very high rate

Since the beginning of the 2000s, several research teams have endeavored to propose a TCP variant that is better adapted to high bandwidth-delay products. Table 5.3 gives a few examples of values used by some TCP variations for the AIMD parameters. The idea is of course to propose values giving the best possible function. The whole difficulty resides in the fact that the solution must preserve fair bandwidth sharing and not be too aggressive towards other flows, regardless of the transport protocol used.

TCP variant	α	β
TCP Reno	1	$\frac{1}{2}$
BIC-TCP	1 or $bin.search$	$\frac{1}{8}$
CUBIC	$cub(cwnd, history)$	$\frac{1}{5}$
HighSpeed TCP	$inc(cwnd)$	$decr(cwnd)$
Hamilton TCP	$f(last_{loss})$	$1 - \dfrac{RTT_{\min}}{RTT_{\max}}$
Scalable TCP	$0.01 * cwnd$	$\frac{1}{8}$

Table 5.3. *Values of AIMD constants used by some TCP variations for large bandwidth-delay networks*

We present these variations in chronological order of appearance.

5.6.1. *HighSpeed TCP*

Proposed by Sally Floyd in 2003, HighSpeed TCP aimed to solve the issue of TCP requiring a long time to recover from a loss event. HighSpeed TCP modifies α and β values by replacing them, respectively, with an increasing function and a decreasing function of the actual size of the congestion window. HighSpeed is therefore capable of adapting and being more aggressive as the link's rate increases.

This function is only activated when the window's size starts exceeding a certain number of packets (38).

5.6.2. *Scalable*

In 2003, Tom Kelly proposed Scalable-TCP, a TCP variant for networks with a very high bandwidth-delay product. It consists of constantly increasing the size of the congestion window without taking into consideration the actual value and decrementing less ($\frac{1}{8}$ instead of $\frac{1}{2}$). Therefore, at constant RTT, Scalable manages to have a constant time between a loss and a return to the value before the loss, regardless of the link's rate (hence its name).

This function is only activated when the window's size starts exceeding a certain number of packets (16).

5.6.3. *BIC-TCP*

BIC-TCP [XU 04] is a TCP variant introduced in 2004 by Injong Rhee. It is designed for networks with a high bandwidth-delay product. As its full name (Binary Increase congestion Control) indicates that during the congestion avoidance phase it adds a mechanism of binary search for the optimum operating point by using two bounds, $W_{\min}$ and $W_{\max}$, that correspond to the last value of the congestion window for which sending did not cause packet loss and to the one corresponding to the last packet loss, respectively. If the upper boundary ends up being exceeded (thus indicating that it is not the maximum), the protocol returns to a phase of faster incrementation of the congestion window (called Max Probing) in order to find a more adequate $W_{\max}$ value.

5.6.4. *H-TCP*

Doug Leith proposed H-TCP in 2004 to try to solve a certain number of problems encountered by HighSpeed TCP and BIC-TCP. The main problem was that these protocols become more aggressive as their congestion window grows, which is a disadvantage for new flows arriving in the system. He suggested solving this by using a function that uses the date of the last loss to modify the increase of the congestion window's size. To reduce the window size in case of loss, it uses the current RTT measurement to modulate the β parameter. Therefore, in a situation where the network's queues are completely saturated (thereby increasing the delay measured), the window will be reduced that much more in order to try to return to a more stable situation.

5.6.5. *CUBIC*

Proposed in 2005 by Injong Rhee, CUBIC [RHE 05] builds upon some of the ideas used in BIC regarding the way it increases the congestion window's size. It does this according to a cubic function – hence its name. A history (based on the date of the last loss) is used to regularly update the size of the congestion window (in a way that is unrelated to the value of RTT). Strictly speaking, CUBIC does not use AIMD.

This TCP variant automatically goes into TCP NewReno mode if the protocol detects that it is in conditions of low bandwidth-delay product.

Table 5.4 gives the parameters of the response function of the TCP variants presented. Figure 5.6 gives the corresponding graphs.

For some variants, like CUBIC, it is not easy to apply this simple model because it was designed to behave as fairly as TCP when the BDP or RTT are low, and more aggressively when it is in the conditions of a network with a high BDP. Some TCP variants use a cutting value that is fixed in number of packets (for example about 30 for HSTCP) to move from a TCP-friendly mode to a high-speed mode where it will try to use the capacities of the network more intensively.

CP variant	C	d
TCP Reno	1.22	0.5
BIC	15.5	0.5
HighSpeed TCP	0.12	0.835
Hamilton TCP	0.12	0.835
Scalable	0.08	1.0

Table 5.4. *Parameters of the response function of some TCP variants,*
$$R = \frac{MSS}{RTT} * \frac{C}{p^d}$$

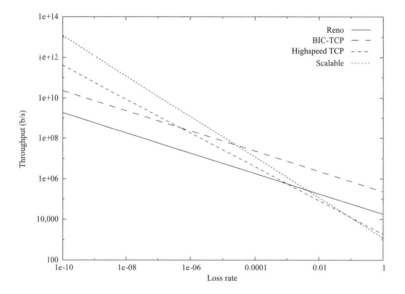

Figure 5.6. *Comparison of the different response functions of some TCP variants*

5.7. Conclusion

Transporting large volumes of information over long distances requires hardware and software configuration of the sending and receiving equipment as well as an adapted transport protocol. This chapter has shown us that obtaining an optimum performance in the context of flow interaction is a technical problem that remains difficult to solve and often necessitates the use of diagnosis and calibration tools such as PATHNIF [GUI 09]. The use of parallel flows is a technique frequently applied by grid users to compensate for the difficulties of parameterization or the deficiencies of certain hardware configurations. The user must nevertheless be conscious of the fact that this approach does not respect the principle of fair bandwidth sharing, which is one of the critical foundations of the Internet. It is therefore advisable to use it only in dedicated high-speed networks. Today high-speed transport protocols having the same fairness and convergence properties as TCP are available. For the most part, they are installed in modern operating systems. They help users to considerably increase performances on the Internet's links, which have very high bandwidth-delay products. Chapter 10 gives examples of TCP configurations and of the system that allow us to obtain adequate transport performances in a high-performance environment.

Chapter 6

Measuring End-to-End Performances

6.1. Objectives of network measurement and forecast in a grid

End-to-end characterization of the links that connect all the sites of a distributed system, and of a grid in particular, aims to enable applications to monitor and improve their performance themselves when transport services are not optimized for machine-to-machine computing and communication. When a distributed application is designed, the designer makes decisions regarding network adaptation and the choice of communication tools to use. Actually, application programmers can develop appropriate optimization strategies and algorithms for both task distribution and communication programming. If they have raw performance measurements or functions synthesizing a network's *cost* based on these measurements, their decisions will be that much more efficient.

Programmers now have a greater knowledge of the semantics of flows and the importance of data movements in the progression of computing. With these measurements, they can better adapt and interleave computing phases and communication phases to overcome the performance problems of the network or its underlying protocols.

It must be noted, however, that while this method, based on adaptation at the application level, is often used in current grids to compensate for the network's weaknesses, it requires more work and expertise from application programmers. It nevertheless remains complementary to the optimizations and adaptations of the network protocols presented in the previous chapters. The purpose of these approaches is to fully exploit the functionalities and specificities of the communication infrastructure and to make things simpler for the users. These approaches are incrementally deployed in distributed environments.

6.1.1. *Illustrative example: network performance and data replication*

Data replication is often used in a grid to provide users and applications with fast and reliable access to data [STO 01]. To this end, instead of having only one storage space, data grids provide replicated data warehouses that are distributed, just like users. Data replication has two main objectives:

– fault tolerance; and

– data-access optimization.

To tolerate file-server faults or copy errors, different data copies are kept on different and remote sites. The optimization of data-access performance aims to minimize the time spent by an end user or its application in reading or writing data on the remote server.

The optimization of replicated-data access covers two aspects:

(1) minimization of response times during data access;

(2) minimization of the time to dynamically create new replicas.

In both cases, the aim is to minimize a response time. In the first case, the main job of optimization is to find a resource that has a copy of the data element requested so that information can be recovered at minimum cost. In the second case, it involves creating new data that are *replicated* from existing data, so that the transfer from the source space to the destination is minimal.

The issue of updates for data synchronization is not taken into account here: the only interest lies in the minimization of transfer time. In the remainder of this section, we assume that replication granularity is at the file level, i.e. the smallest unit of data considered for transfers is a single file, even if the applications can use remote input-output libraries or other primitive libraries to locally or remotely access parts of a file. We also assume that data are partially, rather than completely, replicated. This means that, at any moment, not all of the files are present everywhere.

The problem of replication optimization (also called *best-replica selection*) is described as follows.

Consider the example of a user located at the Fermilab site in the United States who wishes to access file1.dbf, which is reproduced at CERN (in Switzerland), in Italy and France but not at Fermilab. It is assumed that a replication manager implements the replica-selection service and that, at each of the four sites, the same grid middleware is installed.

The Fermilab user sends his request for access to file1.dbf to Fermilab's local replication manager, whose task is to provide the file locally in the Fermilab data warehouse. The replication manager has to first communicate with a catalog of replicas in order to obtain information on the file's physical location before it can then trigger the file transfer.

Three replicas of the requested file exist on three different and remote sites, and the replication manager needs to decide which is the best replica, i.e. the best place to get the file from in the fastest way possible. The best from the user's point of view means that the file requested is created locally with a minimum delay between the request and actual local access to the file. In other words, the *response time* to access file1.dbf must be minimized. This corresponds to minimization of data migration. Therefore the three sites can have storage hardware and network connections with different access times. The replication process from the CERN could take five minutes whereas file transfers from France or Italy could take eight or 10 minutes. In this case, the replica at the CERN is the best location, and a data transfer from the CERN to the Fermilab will be initiated by the replication manager.

In this context, we want large data sets (files) in the order of the mega or gigabyte size, where transfer time has a considerable impact on the performance of a data-intensive application. We must consider a distributed community of users with regard to accessing these files. Even if a remote access mechanism is used, network traffic can be significant and therefore the load, capacity and availability of the network links used during data transfers can significantly lower application performance.

This example illustrates why it can be important for the middleware (here one of its components, called the replication manager) and the users to have information on the performance regarding access to the complex set of interconnected resources, as well as knowledge of the end-to-end transmission capacities on the network. The global cloud network must therefore be characterized by simple and pertinent parameters and its core properties must be measured.

Selecting the best source for reading data requires the characteristics of the path between the destination and each possible source to be forecasted. The exact forecast of the performances obtained for each source requires, in particular, a measurement of the available bandwidth, *both end-to-end and hop-by-hop*, of the latency and of the packet-loss rate.

It can also be interesting to determine whether there would be an advantage in splitting up the copy. For example, the copy of the first half of the file would be done from site B while the parallel copy of the second half of the file would come from site C. To make this decision, information on the performance of each element (*hop*) on the network path is required. If the bottleneck is a link shared by two connections, however, the transfer time cannot be reduced by splitting up the file in this way. For there to be a real interest in data fragmentation, the paths must be disjointed.

Besides this, several works [HAC 02] have shown that the total rate of parallel streams increases on paths with little congestion.

Nevertheless, the effect is reversed and more severe if parallel streams are used on an already-congested path.

Consequently, extra measurements, such as packet delay and loss, can be necessary in order to determine the number of parallel streams that should be used. Even in the case of one single stream, accurate measurements of the network can be used to improve performance and resource allocation.

6.1.2. *Objectives of a performance-measurement system in a grid*

In a vast grid infrastructure, the activity of supervision is essential for the system to function well globally. Network supervision is an important component of this activity and must be harmoniously integrated into it. Indeed, by their very nature, grid infrastructures are distributed and involve many different sites. The correct functioning of the infrastructure is therefore completely dependent on availability of the network connecting the different sites.

Performance tracking is a crucial problem in any network. In general, the performance-tracking system of a network shows the status of the network to the network managers. In the case of grids, this status must also be shown to the end-users. This tracking enables them to effectively choose the best network links at all times.

The main objectives of the supervision, measurement and estimation of the network's performance in a grid environment are:

– the *discovery* and diagnosis of network problems that have an effect on the performance of distributed computing applications;

– the *tuning of network parameters* in order to improve the performance of distributed-computing applications;

– *better use* of the available network capacities;

– the *collection of the data* necessary for providing information on the network's status.

A large number of network-supervision tools are available. The problem is in deploying them wisely in the grid and providing high-performance access to the data collected by these tools [WAH 00]. This general goal implies two distinct tasks:

– the supply and collection of supervision data, which is useful for both the infrastructure's management and applications;

– the means of access to data collected in a useful and usable format.

6.2. Problem and methods

Having identified the *why* of network-performance supervision in a grid and having shown that the spectrum of users was vast – going from the user to the manager and including distributed applications – the problems that are then posed are of the *what* (what exactly must be measured?) and the *how* variety.

Defining a grid's network-measurement architecture requires:

– the choice of *measurement parameters* relevant to the grid's usage context;

– the choice of the *methodology* and tools to carry out the measurement;

– the choice of the *system's architecture* and its integration in the global supervision system;

– the decision of *localization* and strategy for sensor deployment;

– the *scheduling* of sensor measurement and coordination.

The subject of end-to-end measurement of a network has been explored over several years. The Internet Engineering Task Force, via the IP Performance Metrics group [STE 05], as well as national research networks such as GEANT or Internet2 have active programs in place. A framework for Internet protocol (IP) performance metrics and a debate on questions related to network supervision are presented in [PAX 98a, PAX 98c].

The OGF's *Network Measurement* Work Group (NM-WG) identified and explained the characteristics of network performances corresponding to the specific grid context [LOW 04].

Basing our discussion on this document, in the following sections we detail the general principles of network-performance measurement in a grid.

6.2.1. *Terminology*

The OGF's NM-WG defined a common nomenclature of the observations linked to the measurements taken by different systems. The aim of this nomenclature is to enable supervision systems to classify the measurements they take. With this nomenclature, measurements can be grouped according to the methodology used, the characteristics they measure and the entities measured. In general, systems maintain original measurement data as well as synthesized characteristics.

There are two important elements for describing network measurement. The first element is measurement of the characteristic measured. The second element is the network entity that the measurement describes: the path, the hop, etc.

Networks are often represented in the form of graphs, with network entities being divided into nodes and paths. A node does not necessarily correspond solely to a single physical entity, but can represent a range of devices, especially an autonomous system, switch or virtual node. A path is a unidirectional connection from one node to another node and is represented by the ordered pair of end-points. One path exists between the two nodes used as measurement parameters. Figure 6.1 is a UML[1] diagrammatic representation of the main network entities considered in measurement and the relationships between them.

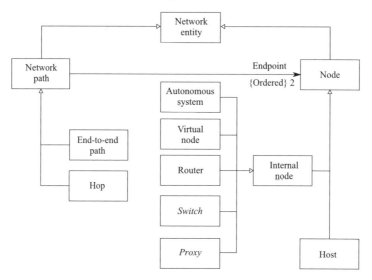

Figure 6.1. *Representation of network entities proposed by the OGF's NM-WG*

Three important terms were defined:

– *network characteristics* are the intrinsic properties of a portion of the network and are linked to the network's performance and reliability;

– *measurement methods* are the methods and techniques of measurement of these characteristics;

– an *observation* is a piece of information obtained by the application of the measurement methodology.

The relationship between these terms is illustrated in Figure 6.2. Many network characteristics are intrinsically hop-by-hop values, whereas most measurement methodologies are end-to-end.

—————————

1. In the UML notation, the arrows with white heads represent a heritage.

Consequently, what is effectively declared by the measurements can be the result obtained for the smallest segment: the *bottleneck*. We distinguish between links (*hop-by-hop*) and paths (*end-to-end*) when required. As illustrated by Figure 6.2, characteristics are applied to network entities. As pointed out above, network entity is a generic term that encompasses nodes, paths and autonomous systems.

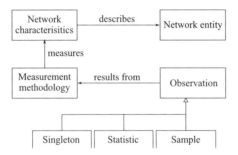

Figure 6.2. *Terminology used by the NM-WG nomenclature*

The three main parts of the system illustrated in Figure 6.2 are:

– *Characteristics*: a characteristic is an intrinsic property that is linked to the performance and reliability of a network entity. More specifically, a characteristic is a primary property of the network or its traffic. A characteristic is the property itself, and not an observation of this property. One example of a characteristic is bottleneck capacity. It is worth noting that a characteristic is not necessarily associated with one unique value. For example, packet loss is an important characteristic of paths. Nevertheless, this loss rate can be expressed as a fraction of all the traffic sent or more specifically as a loss profile with detailed statistical properties.

– *Measurement method*: this is a technique for recording or estimating a characteristic. In general, there are several ways to measure a given characteristic. Raw-measurement methodologies use a technique that gives a direct measurement of the characteristic, while derived-measurement methodologies can be an aggregate or an estimate based on a measurement set. For example, the statistical analysis of packet bursts can be used to estimate the bandwidth capacity.

As an example, let us consider the round trip delay as a characteristic to be measured. It can be:

- measured directly using the *Ping* tool;

- calculated using the transmission time of a Transport Control Protocol (TCP) packet and the reception of the matching ACK; or

- estimated using the information on the links' propagation or the queues' size.

Each of these techniques is different with advantages and drawbacks in terms of exactitude, precision and ease of use.

– *Observations*: a piece of data produced from a measurement methodology is an observation. An observation can be:

- a singleton, which is the smallest personal observation;

- a sample, which is a number of singletons of the characteristic from the same set; or

- a statistic observation, which is derived from a statistic computation on a sample of observations.

A classification of the observations is given in the RFC2330 [PAX 98b]. As network characteristics are very dynamic, temporal information must be associated with each observation recorded. This information indicates on what date the observation was made. For singleton observations, a simple time stamping can suffice. For statistical observations, it is the beginning and the end of the observation time's interval that must be indicated. In general, observations must be recorded with attributes describing the conditions that prevailed at the time of observation.

For certain characteristics, the measurement reports must specify the level of the network layer being studied. Being specific, for throughput measurements, the headers added by each layer must be deduced from the effective bandwidth for the user. In general, measurements are taken at the level of layers 3 and 4 of the Open Systems Interconnection reference model, where layer 1 is hardware support, layer 2 is the data-link layer dealing with the frame's format (e.g. SDH/SONET or Ethernet), layer 3 is the network layer (IP) and layer 4 is the transport layer (e.g. User Datagram Protocol (UDP), Real-time Transport Protocol+UDP, TCP).

Problems related to determining the network entity measured can include:

– the choice of protocol that can influence the network's behavior;

– the different quality of service (QoS) levels that influence all aspects of the network's behavior. In fact, certain QoS policies can specify different links between the same host couple with different traffic levels or classes;

– the instabilities that can mean that the same path end-point experiences a completely different environment at each instant;

– in high-bandwidth environments, hosts often measure the characteristics of the bottleneck, rather than that of the whole network path.

In the next section we detail the characteristics, as well as the measurement methods and tools with which to evaluate them.

6.2.2. *Inventory of useful characteristics in a grid*

This section proposes a standard set of network characteristics and a hierarchical classification of these characteristics that are useful for grid applications and services. The nomenclature and hierarchy presented offer a common dictionary of terms and relations between commonly-used measurements. The hierarchy enables measurements to be grouped depending on the characteristics measured.

Figure 6.3 details the set of metrics. The main ones are:

– the round trip delay;

– the one-way delay'

– the TCP and UDP packet loss;

– the throughput;

– the site's connectivity; and

– the service's availability.

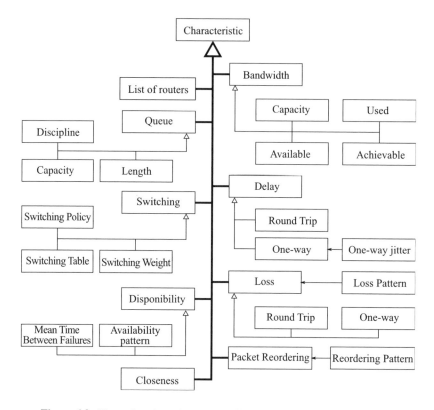

Figure 6.3. *Hierarchy of metrics proposed by the NM-WG group of the OGF*

The bandwidth characteristic is the most important metric for characterizing an end-to-end network service. Bandwidth can be measured as a metric of the usage of a router's aggregated link and as a flow metric associated with a transfer time. Throughput (send bandwidth) is different from goodput (reception bandwidth). The goodput and a portion of the throughput represent the effective bandwidth without protocol information and retransmissions. The available bandwidth of a link can be defined as a function of two other characteristics: capacity and usage. Usage corresponds to the quantity of traffic using the path. The available bandwidth can also be measured directly by injecting traffic into the network.

According to the definitions of the characteristics and of the measurement methods presented above, the available bandwidth is a characteristic because its measurements are not equivalent to those of any other characteristic. This gives it a very specific place in the hierarchy.

goodput: $\overline{g_i} = \frac{1}{T_i} \sum_{t=0}^{T_i} g_i(t)$

aggregate goodput: $G(t) = \sum_{i=1}^{N} g_i(t)$

goodput variation:

$$\sigma_i = \sqrt{\frac{1}{T_i} \sum_{t=0}^{T_i} \left(g_i(t) - \overline{g_i}\right)^2}$$

standard distribution:

$$\left\{ p_{i,k} = p\left(\frac{k}{100} * C_a \leq g_i(t) < \frac{k+1}{100} * C_a\right) \mid k \in [[0; 100[[\right\}$$

aggregate throughput: $X(t) = \sum_{i=1}^{N} x_i(t)$

maximum transfer time: $T_{\max} = \max(T_i)$

average transfer time: $\overline{T} = \frac{1}{N_{\text{forward}}} \sum_{i=1}^{N_{\text{forward}}} T_i$

minimum transfer time: $T_{\min} = \min(T_i)$

transfer time variation:

$$\sigma_{T_i} = \sqrt{\frac{1}{N_{\text{forward}}} \sum_{n=1}^{N_{\text{forward}}} \left(T_i - \overline{T}\right)^2}$$

where g_i is the goodput, T_i the transfer time of the ith file, and N_{forward} corresponds to numbers of files transferred.

6.2.3. *Measurement methods*

To collect the data that enable us to extract end-to-end characteristics, a series of network-supervision tools are available. These tools belong to two families: active probes and passive probes. The next two sections present these two measurement approaches traditionally used in generalist networks and in computing networks in order to understand their behavior and highlight the interactions between applications and the network.

6.2.3.1. *Active method*

Active measurement consists of generating traffic at one point in the network (at one end point or at the core of the network) and injecting it into one or several network paths, then observing the end-to-end effects (i.e. between the generator and the receiver): loss rate, delay, Round Trip Time (RTT), etc.

Active measurements enable the user to measure the characteristics of his network path, from the source to the chosen destination. The main drawback of this approach is its intrusiveness. Measurement traffic, notably introduced for throughput estimation, can be voluminous and introduce a disturbance that causes the network status to evolve and skews the measurement.

Several slightly intrusive techniques have been studied over the last few years. These techniques, which derive throughput from the measurement of a delay variation between consecutive packet pairs (called packet-pair methods), are often unreliable in very-high-speed networks. Consequently, despite their notable intrusiveness, the throughput-measurement methods that fill the pipe to evaluate its width remain widely used in high-speed grids because they are accurate.

6.2.3.2. *Passive method*

Unlike the active approach, the passive-measurement approach is not based on the injection of extra, non-useful traffic into the network. It involves *passively* observing traffic in transit and studying its properties in one or more points of the network.

The advantage of passive measurements is that they are not intrusive and do not change the status of the network. However, it is very difficult to determine end-to-end performance from the pieces of information (the aggregate throughput, the queues' sizes) gathered passively within the network. Still, the passive measurements carried out, notably, on the effective transfers at sender or receiver level can be used for performance forecasts. In this case, for example, it is a matter of keeping a history of the durations of recent file transfers, depending on their volume.

Passive-metrology systems are differentiated depending on the mode of analysis of traces: whether they are measured in real-time or not.

In *real-time* or online analysis, computations are carried out during the time it takes the packet to cross the measurement probe. This approach has the advantage of not necessitating data storage. Since it consumes little network and storage capacity, this method can be used to analyze the network's behavior over very long periods. The statistics are therefore reliable and significant. The authorized computation time being limited, however, so is the complexity of the possible analyses.

In an *offline analysis*, the traffic trace is entirely captured and analysis is carried out later. Such an approach requires enormous storage resources and, consequently, does not allow statistical studies to be carried out on very long traces. On the other hand, an offline analysis allows complex and diversified analyses that lead to a refined traffic characterization.

Passive-measurement probes are often localized in routers. The tools NetFlow and sFlow analyze the traffic moving through the routers and regularly generate statistical information on the average observed throughput during a given time interval. More performant probes, based on network processors or Field-programmable Gate Arrays, enable more fine-grained analyses, packet by packet.

6.2.3.3. *Measurement tools*

Many software tools for network-performance measurement have been proposed in the literature. The Cooperative Association for Internet Data Analysis website regularly inventories them. Here, we only present a few examples of tools, among them most popular and most widely deployed in grid-supervision systems.

The *Ping* tool is an active measurement tool that is frequently used to measure the RTT and the performance loss of a link. Based on the Internet Control Message Protocol, it gives:

– the duration of loops in milliseconds (ms);

– the packet loss in percentages;

– the short-term variability of the response-time (time scale of a second); and

– the lack of accessibility, i.e. the absence of response for a succession of tests.

The *Traceroute* tool is an active measurement tool that gives the list of routers traversed by packets sent up to their destination and gives an indication of the passage time at each of these nodes. Iperf [IPE] is an active tool that is used to measure the maximum TCP or UDP bandwidth that is usable from end to end. *Iperf* is very useful for adjusting diverse TCP parameters. Based on an active method, *Iperf* is a very intrusive method that tries to fill the link with TCP streams in order to measure the maximum throughput of a TCP connection between two points. *Iperf* gives:

– the bandwidth;

– the variation of delay between packets (jitter); and

– the *datagram* losses.

This tool is very often used in grids.

6.3. Grid network-performance measurement systems

Since the beginning of the 2000s, different systems for grid-network supervision have been developed and deployed in grid environments. Among the most well-known are e2emonit [EGE 09], PerfSonar [HAN 05] and Ganglia [MAS 04].

6.3.1. *e2emonit*

e2emonit [EGE 09] is a collection of tools providing end-to-end measurement data. It has been developed within the Datagrid European project (EUD [EUD 01]) and then improved in EGEE-I. It is based on a set of scripts, written in Perl, that control the measurement tools themselves as well as the process of data production and storage for later uses.

The measurement tools included in e2emonit are *Ping*, *Iperf* [IPE] and *udpmon* [JON 06]. These tools enable a certain number of different parameters to be measured:

– the RTT

– the achievable TCP throughput;

– the achievable UDP throughput;

– the packet delay variation; and

– a packet-loss rate.

6.3.2. *PerfSONAR*

PerfSONAR [HAN 05] is a set of services enabling the exchange of supervision data between different network domains. The protocol used for data exchange is based on the diagrams from the OGF's NM-WG. One of the most largely deployed PerfSONAR services today is the measurement-archiving service. It enables us to use data collected from routers and is useful for accurately locating congestion in a network path.

Metric	Tool
Traffic measurement on a link	PerfSONAR
Round trip time	Ping
Packet loss between two *pings*	Ping
Achievable TCP throughput	Iperf TCP
Achievable UDP throughput	udpmon
One-way packet loss	udpmon
Average variation in delay	udpmon

Table 6.1. *Metrics and tools used by PerfSONAR and e2emonit*

Table 6.1 describes the metrics provided by the combination of PerfSONAR and e2emonit.

6.3.3. *Architectural considerations*

The global information service gathers and maintains end-to-end metrics by regularly collecting data from the local monitors. Information systems are based either on Lightweight Directory Access Protocol (LDAP, like Monitoring and Discovery Service [MDS] Globus) or on SQL (like GMA or R-GMA).

Figure 6.4 illustrates the architectural principle of the network-supervision system enabling the acquisition of measurements and their availability to users, as well as its integration in the global supervision system of the grid.

The components of a grid-supervision system must first meet fault-tolerance prerequisites. The faults that can occur in a grid are generally servers going down or a degradation of network performance. The supervision system must allow automatic re-starting of the monitoring servers, duplication or replication of data on other backup servers and, for network aspects, dynamic reconnecting and re-synchronizing of links. The management system for data distributed on the grid adapts to changes in the performance conditions.

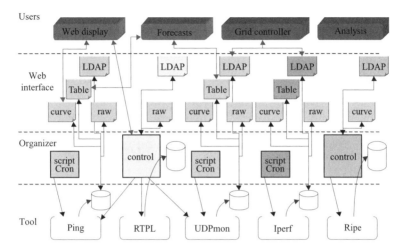

Figure 6.4. *Information system's network sensors*

The dynamic estimation of performance fluctuations must not render data management impossible or inaccessible. All the components of the supervision system are extensible and reusable after a re-dimensioning of the grid's characteristics (number of users and servers).

Data monitoring is generally managed in a distributed way to avoid having a centralized reservoir – a weak point that can threaten the entire grid system. The components (at the level of servers and nodes) must be able to continue to function, even in case of momentary network disconnection. During uses when data are frequently updated, a centralized approach is not satisfactory because a bottleneck can occur (by information streams – statuses, performances, etc. – sent back to the central server). The system components must not be too resource-consuming (CPU, communication, memory and needs) so as not to impact the target machine's performance too greatly.

The choice of data format is important: a compromise is sought between ease of exploitation and performance cost (large ASCII files sent on the network will take up greater bandwidth than compressed files).

Similarly, the monitoring system must have components enabling these transfers to be carried out in a more compact, or partial, way.

Finally, security standards must be respected: use of identification certificates by agents and virtual organizations, encryption of sensitive data transiting the network, etc.

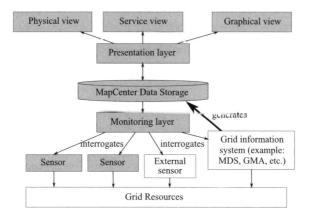

Figure 6.5. *Architecture of the surveillance system of the network for European DataGrid, a precursor of EGEE*

The middleware and the applications access the raw measurements or characteristics estimated and stored in the grid's information system according to a pre-defined process. For example, a *web* service can provide an analysis of packet losses or of the distribution of RTT measurements in charts or tables. The data are also collected at the central level so that daily or monthly statistics can be kept for all sites or for certain selected sites seen from the local monitor point.

Figure 6.5 gives a simplified view of the architecture of the DataGrid supervision system. At the bottom of the figure the different tracking tools, implemented via a set of sensors deployed in each site, are represented. The next layer corresponds to the storage level of measurement data. Data are kept and organized within databases accessible via protocols such as Lightweight Directory Access Protocol or Java Servlet.

In a grid, there are a large number of potential data consumers who, by using a client tool, must be able to access these numerous network-data sources. These constraints have naturally led developers to build access software as *web* services. Network-measurement data are exchanged as eXtended Markup Language (XML) documents.

The mediator (such as MapCenter, represented in Figure 6.6) is a key element of the grid network-measurement architecture. Acting as a central point of contact or portal for clients, the mediator provides a service that enables the available information on measurement data to be discovered. This mediation eliminates the necessity for clients to know the location of monitors, and can be used to keep clients confined to the links around their local monitors.

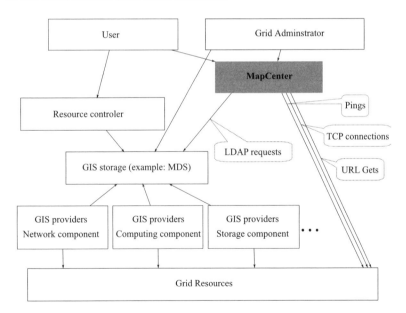

Figure 6.6. *Integration of the mediator in the supervision infrastructure*

6.3.4. *Sensor deployment in the grid*

To create a grid network-supervision system, it is necessary to deploy a set of sensors at each place in the grid. This set of sensors must be capable of representing a large set of computing and storage resources. The sensors, called network-supervision elements, are localized in such a way that they can provide measurements enabling any host machine to find out the conditions of access to any other remote host in the grid. To avoid the active measurements from being too intrusive and to enable the extensibility of the measurement system, it is recommended that the number of sensors and aggregate the measurements be limited.

Therefore, end machines representing the site that are capable of generating tests and collecting measurements are deployed in each site of the grid, as illustrated in Figure 6.7. The data measured are then archived in databases and made available across *web* services.

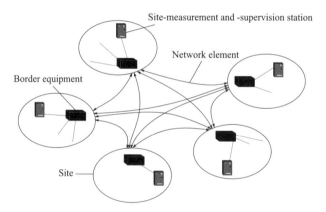

Figure 6.7. *Location of measurement sensors in the grid*

Furthermore, sequencing policies are implemented to control the measurements carried out by each sensor [HAR 05]. For example, in DataGrid's test bench, *Iperf* measurements are initiated every 30 minutes in different time slots for each network-supervision

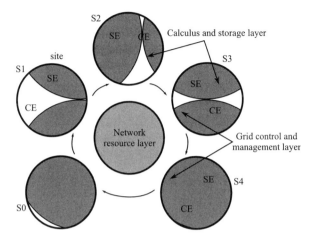

Figure 6.8. *Organization of sensors in a clique within a grid*

element. The data collected by the different tools are locally stored on network-supervision elements. Figure 6.8 shows the principle of round-robin scheduling active measurements.

6.3.5. *Measurement coordination*

As already described in this chapter, a large grid infrastructure needs reliable measurements of the performance of its cloud network. In order to be significant for the performance of real applications, some of these measurements must be carried out from one end to the other: it is the measurement of the performance of an entire network path, from one computer to another. Nevertheless, all these end-to-end measurements, because of their nature, are very intrusive because they consume bandwidth that could be used by applications themselves. In addition to this, in order to obtain reliable measurements, the different measurements must not overlap. For example, if two sites try to measure the achievable bandwidth on a third site at the same time, the result will probably not be so reliable. Therefore, end-to-end measurements must be programmed to take these constraints into consideration. The first e2emonit deployments were manually programmed using "cron" tasks.

This is difficult to maintain, however, and badly handles deployment beyond a handful of sites.

In order to overcome this sequencing problem, a Probes Coordination Protocol (PCP) software was proposed [HAR 05] and was deployed in the EGEE grid (EGE [EGE 04]). PCP enables sequencing of activities that must occur at the level of a site or a set of sites. An activity is generally a script or an executable, for example the execution of a measurement probe. A set of sites constitutes a clique. A particular site can be a member of several cliques at a time, as illustrated in Figure 6.9.

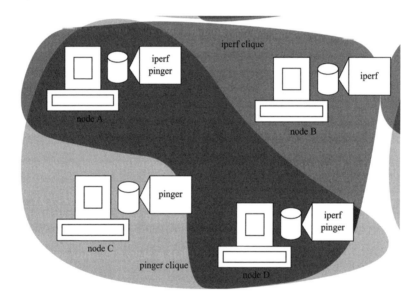

Figure 6.9. *Recording of the same sensor in several cliques*

Programming is carried out by inserting a token around the clique: a site will only launch an activity if it is in possession of a token (see Figure 6.10). When it executes an activity the token is locked, thus reducing the possibility of measurements overlapping. The token defines the activity that must be executed and enables two independent

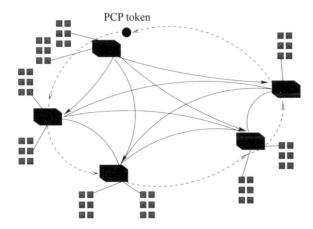

Figure 6.10. *Example of the injection of a clique token in a grid*

periods to be specified. The first of them is the period between each execution of an activity on a particular site and the second is the delay in this activity being executed on different sites. A specific protocol was defined to synchronize the different cliques, as represented in Figure 6.11.

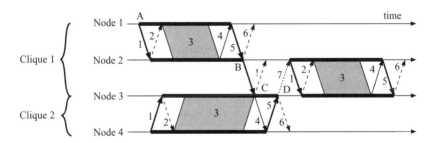

Figure 6.11. *Principles of the inter-clique protocol*

It must be noted that PCP also provides measurements on demand. In this case, the token presented must specify that the supervision probe must be executed without delay, while no other site is involved in the clique. Once the probe has been executed, the token is deleted from the site. In addition, although designed for the execution of supervision probes, PCP can be used to program or synchronize all types of distributed activity.

6.4. Performance forecast

Several efforts have been made in the grid community to better predict bulk data transfer delays using the network's characteristics [CHE 02, VAZ 01, WOL 99].

6.4.1. *The Network Weather Service tool*

The *Network Weather Service* or NWS [WOL 98] is certainly the most well-known forecast tool in computing networks. It proposes a general architecture for measuring and predicting performance in distributed-computing environments. NWS gives performance forecasts for the network as well as the processor and storage elements. Its forecast models are based on estimates of the available bandwidth, calculated from chronological series gathered by frequent active measurements. NWS seeks a good balance between precision and the low intrusiveness of probes. Many forecast methods can be applied to these time series. The originality of NWS is that it dynamically evaluates a certain number of methods and chooses the most appropriate one on-the-fly.

The characteristics of NWS are the following:
– low intrusiveness;
– longevity of execution;
– precision of forecasts;
– ubiquity.

The NWS system is based on four different components:

– a name server (*NWS-name-server*) that records all the system's entities (memory components, sensors, prediction functions and measurement tasks). It is a central source of information for the system;

– a memory service (*NWS-memory*) that safeguards all measurements in a circular queue and delivers them on demand;

– a forecast service (*NWS-forecaster*) that constitutes the computing core of the predictions of the NWS system;

– sensors (*NWS-sensor*) that correspond to the measurement processes carrying out all the measures.

A sensor runs on each of the supervised sites and provides measurements of the CPU used, available CPU, memory and hard disk, as well as the network. Network measurements are the TCP throughput, connection time and latency (TCP throughput, TCP connect-time, TCP latency). To get the highest precision without overloading the machines and the network too much, the NWS sensors use a combination of passive and active measurement methods.

NWS was designed to be the least intrusive possible. Thus, its CPU use is limited to 3%, its memory use to 3 MB and its disk use depends on the number of measurement series but is in the order of 20 MB.

For measurement coordination, two modes are proposed:

– a periodic regime in which experiments are periodically launched, with a definite periodicity; or

– a regime in clique, in which the experiments are sequenced in such a way that in a given time interval there is at most only one single ongoing experiment. The clique protocol operates on the basis of a token exchanged between the sites measured (see PCP).

NWS proposes a distributed data-storage system. Each *NWS-memory* process is registered, along with all the measurement series of a given period, to the *NWS-name-server*. This enables data to be accessed later on, without necessarily knowing where they are recorded.

The aim and main originality of the NWS system is prediction (*NWS-forecast*). This forecaster generates short-term estimates. NWS embeds a series of forecast methods that are dynamically chosen depending on the forecast error obtained in each context. *NWS-forecast* provides a programming interface that allows us to add new forecast methods as well as a set of functions to include calls to the estimator from within an application.

In [PRI 02], the precision of NWS forecasts was studied on a real grid network. It turns out that NWS underestimates the actual TCP throughput in high-speed environments, but gives good predictions in very loaded or weakly provisioned environments. NWS therefore cannot be used for bulk data transfers in a high-performance grid but brings good results in an environment that is averagely provisioned.

Another performance-forecast approach was put forward in [VAZ 01]. It is based on performance information of previous real transfers, collected by the instrumented GridFTP application and not on active measurements. This passive method that exploits real results is therefore less intrusive for the network. The instrumentation of applications and the trace collection can load the computing end points. Furthermore, traces depend on the actual activity of the grid. Traces therefore do not constitute regular time series on which robust statistical analyses are carried out. This method can provide acceptable values if the network's activity is regular. If not, the forecasts are unreliable. This is the reason for which, in production grids, a forecast service rigorously exploiting network-measurement data is implemented. We describe this in the next section.

6.4.2. *Network-cost function*

The different measurement systems presented in the previous sections gather and publish pertinent and detailed tracking information in the grid's global information system, like MDS [CZA 01] or R-GMA [BYR 02]. Nevertheless, in order to optimize application performance, a component of grid middleware – such as the replication management seen in our introductory example – needs global and simple estimates of *transfer costs* between two defined end point machines.

Basing our discussion on the proposed network-supervision infrastructures, an independent service in charge of supplying an estimate of network performance on demand was defined. This service was studied in the DataGrid project and then deployed in the EGEE production grid.

Let us consider the following example. Given a site source, *src*, two destination sites, *dest1* and *dest2*, and a quantity of data to transfer, *volume*, the effective data transfer time is obtained by the formula:

$$TT_i = \text{volume}/x_i$$

with TT_i being the transfer time and x_i the goodput between *src* and $dest_i$.

These linear relations enable the estimation of transfer time in advance by estimating the useful throughput between *src* and $dest_i$ that the application will obtain at the time of transfer.

With X_1 and X_2 the TCP throughputs of links 1 and 2 representing, respectively, end-to-end paths $(src, dest1)$ and $(src, dest2)$, the cost function, f, for each destination can be expressed as a transfer delay, i.e.:

$$f(dest1) = \left(\text{volume}/X_1\right)$$
$$f(dest2) = \left(\text{volume}/X_2\right).$$

In this particular scenario, comparing $f(dest1)$ and $f(dest2)$ from the source *src* becomes possible.

6.4.3. *Formulating the cost function*

The *transfer cost* function is calculated from the systematic raw measurement of network performances. This approach provides a robust network-forecast service that can be used to improve the grid's resource management or the applications' execution. Such a service simplifies the exploitation of network-supervision data by users. It has also been shown that certain approximations are useful in certain cases. They allow a good balance between precision, efficiency and evolutivity. In general, it is possible to define an abstract cost for each type of network transfer. This cost can be expressed in the form of a time necessary for transferring a dataset, or an access time in the case of an interactive session. It can also represent a real cost in the case of a business session.

The formula for the function that expresses the *network cost* is therefore different depending on context and demand. This function can take on a simple form in the case of bulk data transfers or be more complex in the case of a combination of interactive data and large transfers carried out using interconnections provided by a commercial network. Since the set of possible functions is large and the context widened, the network cost-estimate service, as well as its interface, are open and extensible.

The ultimate goal of a network-cost estimate function is to provide a simple service with variable input and output parameters. It must also derive performance forecasts with variable precision. This network service is connected to the grid's network-supervision infrastructure and information system at the same time. It provides an extensible application programming interface (API) and an open framework for accessing the different data-publication services such as LDAP/MDS, R-GMA or a *web* service.

A network-cost estimate service was developed in DataGrid projects and in EGEE. It is interfaced with several data sources. The dedicated API enables the function to be called directly using optimization tools. This API offers an initialization function to implement service parameters: the type and localization of the information service, the estimate function and input parameters, as well as a generic call to access the estimation value.

For example, the function NetworkCost (SrcSE, DestSE, file-size) carries out the following steps:

– recovery of the source and destination addresses of the sensor representing the site:

(1) $SourceNM = Map(SourceSE)$,

(2) $DestNM = Map(DestSE)$;

– collection of the set of supervision data required:

(3) $NMdata = Collect(CostFunctionType, SourceNM, DestNM)$;

– invocation of the estimate process and return of the result:

(4) $E2Ecost = CostFunction(NMdata, file\text{-}size)$.

6.4.4. *Estimate precision*

The precision required for cost estimation depends on what the result is to be used for. For example, to compare two destinations, as in our previous scenario, a classification of the transfer times estimated using data from local representatives will suffice. In certain cases, though, more precise transfer-time estimates will need to be compared.

In the case of bulk data transfer, the effective bandwidth the user will obtain strongly depends on low-level parameters or network conditions that are difficult to control, as we showed in Chapter 5, such as:

– the transport protocol used for the actual transfer;

– the size of the window if the transport protocol used is TCP;

– the number of parallel flows, for example when GridFTP is used;

– the network's load during transfer.

All these factors are examined in Chapter 5 as well as in [HAC 02, MIL 00]. This dependence on the set of low-level parameters makes the design of a generic estimate function very difficult. It is to counter this difficulty – while preserving evolutivity, non-intrusiveness and precision – that a modular architecture was chosen for the design of this service. This modular design enables the progressive integration of new forecast functions, characteristics, active or passive sensors and processing processes.

6.5. Conclusion

Supervision of the network's status and performance turns out to be a very important functionality for grids. Indeed, as the number of potential sources is very high, the absence of such a global network-measurement service can lead to a significant and useless overload of the system and network if users want to estimate performance by themselves. A service mutualizing measurements generally relies on the metrology research and tools coming from the general context of IP networks. The multipoint and multidomain context of grids requires us to consider the location of the sensors and information storage spaces, as well as measurement coordination.

This chapter developed the problems and solutions deployed in current grids for the measurement and analysis of the grid network's performance so that applications and middleware components can exploit it optimally. The solutions proposed here are open and extensible. They can adapt to the future evolutions of network services, particularly to on-demand bandwidth or QoS services. The system of measurement and estimation of the network's performance completes the grid's global supervision system and provides the general information system with dynamic information. Furthermore, the regular collection and storage of measurement information enables us to calculate estimates that are simple to use and relatively reliable.

Chapter 7

Optical Technology and Grids

Chapter 4 showed us how cluster-network technology has been influenced by the use of these infrastructures and, in particular, by the programming models adopted by applications programmers. Contrary to Internet applications that adapt – to some extent – to a best-effort network, parallel applications executed on clusters are optimized by their programmers to take full advantage of the hardware. Chapter 5 exposed the limits of the current programs to address the demands of grid applications and detailed the main alternatives adopted today in these environments. The evolutions of wide-area-network technology and, particularly, optical networks gives us a glimpse not only of an explosion in the capacities of future networks but also of the deployment of new services. These services, very much adapted to the resource-mutualization paradigm as defined in grids but also intrinsically in computing clouds, could significantly improve the network's flexibility and quality of service (QoS).

This chapter presents the state of the art of optical technologies and, in particular, the existing solutions for making the network dynamically reconfigurable and able to provide bandwidth services on-demand or by advanced reservation. Such services, breaking network transparency as well as the hermetic-layer model, could – similarly to the services offered by cluster networks – offer grid-application programmers the personalization functionalities necessary to execute and optimize their very diverse applications.

Section 7.1 of this chapter introduces the different switching paradigms used for optical communications. Section 7.2 deals with the functional aspects of transport networks and their classification in processing planes. Section 7.3 presents the unification of switching paradigms and communication technologies thanks to unified control planes. Using these technical elements, in Chapter 8 we present the mechanisms that are proposed to provide grid users with a bandwidth-on-demand service.

7.1. Optical networks and switching paradigms

7.1.1. *Optical communications*

The development of lasers since the 1960s, associated with the discovery that attenuation in optical fibers could be reduced, has made optical communications possible. Signal mitigation is now less than that observed in coaxial cables. The bandwidth that can be obtained on optical fibers is also greatly superior to such cables. In September 2006, Japanese company NTT carried out a 14 Tbit/s transmission over a distance of 160 km on a single fiber [NTT 09]. In addition, whereas there can be interferences between electric signals passing in different cables, optical signals do not interfere with each over. This enables a large number of fibers to be grouped and installed together between buildings, countries and even continents.

The packet-switching paradigm has been used in traditional data networks because of the scarcity of resources and bandwidth. With the increase in communication capacities offered by optical technology, this problem has become null and void. Nevertheless, this immense optical capacity has raised new problems. In fact, it is the software processing of these communications at the end points (sender and receiver, see Chapter 6) as well as at the intersection points (routers) that have become the bottleneck. Processing an exponential number of packets poses a true challenge regarding the speed of access to a piece of equipment's memory and its energy consumption.

We note here that the high-performance problems analyzed in Chapter 4 are moved to the network's internal equipment. The solutions proposed in clusters could, to some extent, apply to long-haul optical networks.

Although the optical packet-switching paradigm has been studied for about 10 years, the current state of the art does not allow its implementation in production networks. The tendency is to avoid data processing on intermediate network elements by as much as possible and to try to establish end-to-end optical connections. In the absence of packets and optical bursts, this approach implies a return to circuits for data networks or at least for their support. Indeed, the current transport networks are organized into layers of transmission technologies and the circuits can be used in the lower layers to provide reservable resources in order to transmit packets to the upper layers.

Before describing the different optical-switching paradigms, we will review the key components of optical communication technologies that enable the deployment of large capacities in the networks of today and tomorrow.

7.1.1.1. *Wavelength multiplexing*

The digital data produced by distributed applications are processed by electronic devices and are therefore available in the form of electric signals. To transmit them via optical fibers, they must be converted into optical signals. An optical signal is a light wave that propagates along the fiber that acts as a waveguide. The optical transmission operation is carried out by a *transceiver*. A laser emitting in a very narrow waveband at a very high speed and with great precision is normally used to send the optical signal. It is a reverse process at the receiving end based on a photodiode that converts light into an electric signal. The sending and receiving devices are the most costly elements of the optical-transmission chain.

Data are encoded according to a *channel code* that defines how a *bit* (or a group of bits) is represented by the optical signal.

To increase the efficiency of optical fibers, the wavelength-division multiplexing (WDM) technique was introduced about 15 years ago. It is a multiplexing method used to transport several different optical signals on one single fiber. The frequency grid (central wavelength of each channel and channel spacing) is defined by ITU-T [G.602]. For example, the dense WDM (DWDM) technology allows up to 160 channels. Coarse WDM (CWDM) is a more economical version with a larger waveband that tolerates greater frequency dispersion. It has 18 wavelengths, each with a capacity of 2.5 Gbit/s.

In addition to an immense capacity, the WDM technology now also offers all-optical switching across the entire network. This contributes to reducing the latency induced by the O-E-O (optical-electric-optical) conversions. The switching is done by optical add-drop multiplexers (OADMs).

7.1.1.2. *Optical add-drop multiplexers*

An OADM or a *reconfigurable OADM* is a device composed of two different types of input ports and the same two output ports. These ports are fibers with WDM signals and isolated signals on wavelengths.

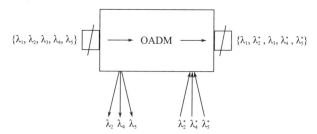

Figure 7.1. An optical add-drop multiplexer

As its name indicates, an OADM has two functions: *add* and *drop*. Figure 7.1 shows an OADM that extracts three lambdas (λ_2, λ_4, and

λ_5) from a fiber and replaces them wihe λ_2^*, λ_4^*, and λ_5^*, while the others are simply transmitted. Its core function is to extract some of the wavelengths of a WDM signal, *drop* them, from the WDM signal's point of view, and replace them with a new signal (*add* function). This device is the cornerstone of all-optical networks. The extracted wavelengths can then be *terminated* on optical receivers and converted into electric signals or injected into a different fiber.

7.1.1.3. *Optical cross-connect*

Optical Cross-Connect (OXC) is the optical equipment that enables network operators to interconnect fibers and control wavelength switching in the network. Different sub-categories exist. If the OXC uses only OADM, it is said to be *transparent* because there is no O-E-O conversion, the OXC is independent of the network protocols. If the OXC is composed of transceivers and an electric switching matrix, the OXC is said to be *opaque* because it can only forward the signals of protocols it understands. Figure 7.2 shows an OXC with two input and two output ports. The two OADMs enable the extraction of wavelengths that are switched in the switching matrix before being injected in a new fiber or terminated.

The OXCs being composed of input or output ports or fibers – which themselves contain wavelengths – require *control* to indicate which wavelength must be switched to a specific output wavelength.

The resulting configuration is a match between inputs and outputs in the bipartite graph. This configuration can be set for varying durations. The timescale defines the switching paradigm:
- shortest duration: optical packet switching (OPS);
- average duration: optical burst switching (OBS);
- longest duration: optical circuit switching (OCS).

These paradigms are detailed in the next section.

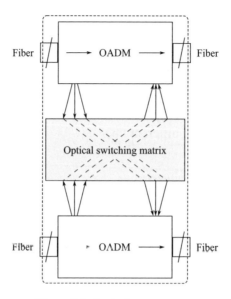

Figure 7.2. *Optical cross-connect*

7.1.2. *Optical switching paradigms*

Three different switching paradigms has been proposed for optical communications.

7.1.2.1. *Optical packet switching*

With OPS, data are transmitted in a non-connected mode and routing decisions are taken at each node [YAO 00]. This is similar to the Internet Protocol (IP), except that it is done exclusively in the optical domain.

This paradigm is not currently implemented in commercial equipment because optical memory does not exist and it is difficult to process the header without any way of storing the payload. To overcome this, some of the mechanisms proposed for burst technology (OBS) use a signal message that is similar to a header and sent in advance of the data. Furthermore, it is also very difficult to switch packets without having buffer memory to absorb load variations.

7.1.2.2. *Optical burst switching*

In the next two models, OBS and OCS, signalization is used to warn network equipment that data will follow.

OBS [QIA 99] was proposed with different signaling mechanisms. Some use *one-way signaling* and others use signaling with acknowledgement. In the first case, a *blockage* can occur in any switch because nothing guarantees the availability of resources nor the capacity to place data in the buffer memory between sender and receiver.

This led [ZAL 09] to propose the classification of switching paradigms into either OBS "if blocking is possible [in a switch]" or into OCS "if no blocking is possible". Let us note that signaling can occur *in-band* or *out-of-band* if the signaling message is sent on a different channel to that of the data. According to this classification, the *tell-and-wait* [WID 95] signaling mechanism for OBS and the wavelength-based routing for OCS are part of the OCS category, to which we will return in section 7.1.2.3.

The *tell-and-go* mechanism [VAR 97] sends signaling messages just before the data and thus requires a buffer at the routers. *Just-enough-time/just-in-time* [ACQ 08] sends the signal with an advance that depends on the number of hops, so that the signaling and configuration can be done before the data reach the equipment. Nevertheless, since the sender does not wait for a reception acknowledgement before sending data, there is a risk of blocking at each switch due to potential contention with another competing stream. In this configuration, the signal message is sent sufficiently in advance to configure the switching matrix of each intermediate router. *Horizon* and LAUC-VF [XIO 00] add the length of the burst and the delay between the signal and the data so that the routers have a schedule of the future use of their resources.

7.1.2.3. *Optical circuit switching*

OCS systematically uses *two-way signaling* and therefore waits for an acknowledgement before sending data. This acknowledgement can be two-way and involve a round trip between the source and the destination, in a manner similar to Resource Reservation Protocol (RSVP), or one-way, coming from a centralized broker.

According to the classification presented in the previous section, the OCS paradigm groups the sharing solutions where data cannot be blocked at the switch. Manually-established static optical circuits belong to this category, and so do dynamically established circuits because data cannot be *blocked* in a switch.

To ensure that data will not be blocked at the switch, two-way signaling mechanisms must be used to make sure that every switch is fine with this *circuit* before sending data. The configuration process is called *lambda-path setup*. A reciprocal process, called *tear down*, is used for the *release* of the circuit.

The selection of the switches used to establish a circuit can be made at each hop, as in [WID 95], or by using source routing. This type of network is therefore relatively easy to control as exogenous sharing decisions can be taken into account and it is possible to decide the path that will be used to create a circuit. This enables *traffic engineering* or on-demand bandwidth brokerage, depending on whether control is given to internal or external customers. In addition, *call admission control* can be applied to these requests.

This controllability makes optical circuits associated with *time-division multiplexing*, such as SONET (*Synchronous Optical NETworking*) or SDH, (*Synchronous Digital Hierarchy*), key components of current *transport networks* [ELL 05]. Despite this, control has its drawbacks. It is necessary to collect and distribute information, make decisions and send signaling messages. All these functions are now well determined, and the complexity of managing such networks has been diluted in the functional planes of transport networks.

7.1.3. *Conclusion*

A few figures and key properties of the three switching paradigms are given in Table 7.1, inspired by [NOR 03].

	OCS	OBS	OPS
Suitable transfer size	> Gb	Dozens of kB	Size of an IP packet
Bandwidth guarantee	Yes	No	No
Possible blocking	At setup	At each switch	At each switch

Table 7.1. *Brief comparison of the OPS, OBS and OCS paradigms*

Today, commercial equipment only supports optical circuits. OBS, and therefore OPS, are technologies envisioned for the future but are not yet used in the production networks of computing grids or clouds. Many of the optical networks in operational today are static. The configuration of the switching points has often been done manually. To meet the frequently changing needs of the grid's users, however, dynamically reconfigurable OCS networks are being deployed in the networks of public and private operators.

Let us note that the dynamically reconfigurable OCS paradigm is similar to the *public switched telephone networks* that have been in use for decades. The main difference comes from the nature of the end-to-end signals exchanged: OCS uses optical signals; while the telephone network uses electrical signals.

7.2. **Functional planes of transport networks**

Dynamically reconfigurable OCS networks are of great interest in the computing grids and clouds sector. Their implementation necessitates a sophistication of the control of these networks. To understand how this control could be transferred to the user or grid middleware, we must first study the different functional planes of a transport network and locate the different control functions of a network.

In [G.800], ITU-T gives the following definition of *transport network*: the functional resources of the network that convey user information between different locations.

Transport networks are divided along three axes: (i) authoritative boundaries; (ii) technology layers; and (iii) functional planes.

The authoritative boundaries limit the extent of the part of the network under a given authority: this is usually called a *domain*. Each network provider can have several domains with different technologies, aims or types of customers. The domains are, in general, interconnected with other domains. The division between domains is called *partitioning*.

A layer is defined by the technology used and groups the equipment or agents that can convey data from one piece of equipment or agent to another. Within a domain, different technology layers can coexist: this is the layering of transport networks. Let us consider an IP/ Multi Protocol Label Switching (MPLS)-over-Ethernet network that uses SONET circuits on an optical physical layer (i.e. fibers) and coarse wavelength division multiplexing (CWDM) as the multiplexing technology. In this example, the layers are IP, MPLS, Ethernet, SONET, CWDM and L1 fibers.

Each technology brings its constraints, control and management properties. In addition to this, and in a functional vision of the transport network, the functional planes define the local organization of the functions that the network accomplishes, and that can be used to use and control it. This model is normally composed of three planes: the *data plane* (or *transmission plane*) is in charge of data transmission; the *control plane* provides the information and functions for the configuration of the data plane by handling the routing aspects; and finally the *management* plane accomplishes monitoring tasks (for example, the protection of certain circuits or traffic engineering) to improve the operational performance or collect statistics. Figure 7.3 represents a domain with its functional planes. These planes can be seen as groups of functions carrying out operations at different timescales.

At one end of this scale is the data plane, which runs transmission operations: it takes $12\,\mu s$ to send a 1,500-byte packet on a 1 Gbit/s Ethernet link. The timescale of the control plane is greater because routing information is less volatile and used for traffic aggregates composed of many packets. Finally, the timescale of management operations is in the order of minutes for recovery following failure, and can take an hour or month for network evolution planning.

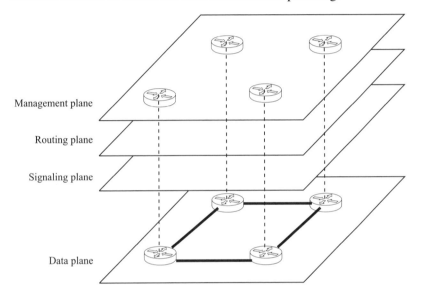

Figure 7.3. *Network with its functional planes: management plane, control plane (signaling plane and routing plane) and data plane*

The next three sections will describe these planes, before going into the details of the control plane, using generalized multi protocol label switching (GMPLS) as the example of a unified control plane.

7.2.1. *Data plane*

The data plane is for *forwarding* the data along a *trail*, i.e. an end-to-end connection that can be used by a client and is composed of *network connections*.

The transmission process can, potentially, necessitate a move from one layer to the other (for example, IP packets inserted in SONET frames). This is done by *adaptation* and *termination*. Adaptation describes how to adapt the data from one layer to the other and termination adds information so that the adapted data can be transmitted to the destination layer. The reverse process is carried out at the destination.

7.2.2. *Control plane*

The data plane is configured using the control plane. This requires the execution of signaling and routing functions, which are sometimes referred to as the *signaling plane* and *routing plane*, respectively.

7.2.2.1. *Routing*

This refers to the process of distributing routing information, i.e. the connectivity and the attributes of links, such as distance, capacity or any information that can be used to compute a path.

7.2.2.2. *Signaling*

Once a path has been determined, signaling is the process of distributing the information to be able to forward the data. In circuit-switched approaches, it can be the distribution of the configurations of switches on the selected path. This process can also inform the source that this configuration is not possible, for example because of competition on the selected path.

7.2.3. *Management plane*

The *International Organization for Standardization* (ISO) proposed the *Fault, Configuration, Accounting, Performance, Security* (FCAPS) management model for telecommunications networks. FCAPS was then refined by ITU-T in [M.300b].

Fault management handles alerts, fault detection and network recovery following failure. Configuration management is responsible for network provisioning (preparing the network to serve the customers), resource discovery, backup and restoration. It coordinates the addition, modification or removal of equipment or resources. Accounting management tracks service usage. Performance management collects statistics for reporting and deals with problems linked to the general network performance. Finally, security management takes care of protecting the network from unauthorized users. It includes user authentication and authorization through the use of permissions, admission rules and activity logs.

ITU-T G.872 [G.801b] concentrates on optical transport networks. It defines the following management capacities:

– *connectivity supervision*, to monitor the integrity of connection routing;

– *signal-quality supervision*, to ensure the performance of connections;

– *protection control*, to manage the protections ($1 + 1$ or $m : n$) of connections. $1 + 1$ means that each line is doubled with a backup line. With an $m : n$ protection, m is used as a backup for n lines.

Finally, *operational support systems* must be mentioned: they are the elements of the architecture that handle the management aspects for a telecommunications service provider. Closer to the customers, the *business support system* manages the products, customers, the revenues, and orders. Both operate closely together.

In the *telecommunications management network* model of the ITU-T [M.300a], network management as defined above is not the only component. It is accompanied by business management or service management, among others. The whole defines the core functionalities needed to operate a network and supply customers.

The *TeleManagement Forum*, an international organization for service providers and suppliers of the communications industry, provides a framework on which to build interoperable operational support systems.

7.2.4. *Conclusion*

As seen in this section, the networks and functional representation of transport networks are described in a functional way by the telecommunications industry, their standardization organization and the Internet Standardization Organization. The configuration of equipment to provide a service is part of this and occurs in the control plane, but provisioning is a management function.

7.3. Unified control plane: GMPLS/automatic switched transport networks

In the previous section, we described the environment of the control plane and, to a lesser extent, the functions it implements. This section describes the functions and protocols used in *unified control planes* such as GMPLS [FAR 05] or automatic switched transport networks (ASTN). Section 7.3.1 presents the *generalized label-switching* approach as an extension of MPLS and section 7.3.2 presents the protocols that make up the GMPLS architecture. The extension towards multidomains is then presented, as are the architectural models of GMPLS networks.

7.3.1. *Label-switching*

Let us recall that MPLS is a transmission mechanism that can be used to create circuits based on IP packets, and thus avoid the usual per-packet routing process. These circuits are called *label switched paths* (LSP). Similarly to OCS, since it is also a circuit, the switches' configuration must be deployed. This configuration informs each switch that the MPLS packets entering with a certain label must leave the switch through a predefined port, with a given new label. The configuration is distributed on the path by RSVP (a reservation protocol) [BRA 97]. MPLS manages label *stacking*, which enables the encapsulation of circuits in other circuits. It has been generalized to technologies other than IP.

It is worth noting that many things can be used as labels, e.g. wavelength, MPLS label, *slot number* in a *time multiplexing* technology (for example SONET) or an Ethernet *virtual local area network* (*VLAN*) label. It should be noted, too, that an order in these multiplexing solutions is possible. This order is given by the hierarchy of the switching types: packet switching, layer-2 switching (for example *VLAN* or ATM), time-division multiplexing wavelength switching, and fiber. It is observed that, in GMPLS, stacking can occur on different layers. In GMPLS, LSPs have a guaranteed bandwidth.

ITU-T proposes a similar architecture to automatically provide a transport service: ASTN/Automatically Switched Optical Network [G.801a]. The following sections describe the protocols of the GMPLS control plane in detail before presenting the extension towards multidomains, then the different architectural models that have been proposed that use GMPLS.

7.3.2. *Protocols: OSPF-TE/RSVP-TE/LMP/PCEP*

GMPLS equipment is broken down into two parts: a switching matrix of one or several of the switching capabilities mentioned above, and their instantiation of the following protocols. This makes up part of the control plane. Routers exchange information via a traditional IP network.

GMPLS is made up of the following three protocols:

(1) open shortest path first (OSPF)-TE [KOM 05] is an extension of OSPF, a protocol for routing-information diffusion. This extension is considered to be *traffic engineering* because it helps during traffic-management operations, such as *traffic grooming*. This OSPF can have two types of elements: *TE-Links* and *TE LSPs*. The former describe the resources that can be used to transmit data: a fiber with the wavelengths it can transmit and how many of them are available, a SONET OC-48 line and its *time slots*, etc. TE LSPs are LSPs presented as TE-Links. This means that they can be used by new LSPs of a higher order in the hierarchy of switching capabilities. It is then easy, using

the OSPF-TE Link-State database, to compute a path using *constrained shortest-path first* (CSPF) by eliminating links that do not satisfy the constraints and by computing the shortest path in the resulting graph. Other path-computing methods can also be used.

(2) RSVP-TE [KOM 04] is the RSVP extension that enables LSP to be created in GMPLS, with *Explicit Route Object* describing the list of routers that must be crossed. Two-way signaling is then carried out using PATH/RESV messages;

(3) *The Link Management Protocol* (LMP) is used for parameter negotiation between neighboring routers that share a TE-Link. It also enables fault-detection, such as a *loss of light*.

Actually, each of these three protocols has an alternative defined in the GMPLS architecture, but these are the most common.

OSPF-TE broadcasts the routing information, so GMPLS can only be used in one domain for reasons of confidentiality and extensibility. The routers on the edges of this domain that adapt the traffic entering or leaving from another network are called *label edge routers* whereas the internal routers are called *label switching routers*.

To provide a path-computing service to entities outside of the domain, the *path computation element* (*PCE*) [FAR 06] was proposed. This computing entity, being part of the domain, receives OSPF-TE messages and can therefore maintain the OSPF-TE database. The PCE can be used to compute an inter-domain path. The *PCE Communication Protocol* (PCEP) [VAS 09] can be used to contact a PCE and ask it to compute a path.

The PCE suffers from many defects and imperfections. Due to the asynchronous nature of the database-updating process, when several paths are requested from PCE at the same time, or if new LSPs have been signaled and PCE has not yet been updated, the paths given by PCE can interfere with each other and not be possible at the same time. Another problem is the difficulty in computing a path to a node that is outside the PCE's visibility. A lot of development is being done on the PCEP. It is increasingly being used in operator networks.

In traditional IP networks, there is no PCE. Each domain uses OSPF for its intra-domain routing, and *Border Gateway Protocol* (BGP) for the inter-domain routing. BGP, as a *path-vector protocol*, announces routes and not link states. Routes between domains can then be used to determine where to go to reach a given destination. Intra-domain routing instances are used to determine paths within domains.

7.3.3. *GMPLS service models*

A *service model* is the description of how a user, or another GMPLS domain, can use the resources of a GMPLS domain. GMPLS was designed with three models in mind: the *peer model*; the *overlay model*; and the *hybrid model*.

In the peer model, the upper layer is supposed to have complete access to the routing information from the lower layers. Likewise, the signaling messages are supposed to be able to move from one end of the network interconnection to the other. In this model, the LSP – which might have been triggered in the lower layer, once established – is presented as a TE-LSP. Therefore, the remaining capacity can be used by new requests from the upper layers. This model nevertheless has a major drawback: privacy. Networks must expose their internal structures as well as the availability of their resources to their peers.

The overlay model is closer to the customer/provider relationship model in the sense that the domains are distinct and do not exchange information, apart from via a *service interface*. In this model, the LSP can be stitched to another network at the boundaries of each domain to create a single end-to-end circuit.

The hybrid model is a mix of the two previous ones: privileged peers have access to some information and control facilities that normal users cannot use. Normal users have to use a different interface to mandate an agent to provision circuits on their behalf. This motivates the existence of several interfaces to access a domain's control plane: the *network-to-network interface* (NNI) and the *user-to-network interface* (UNI) [SWA 05].

7.3.4. *Conclusion*

We saw in this section, that control facilities that unify multiplexing technologies through label switching have been proposed. They are domain-centric and cannot scale as-is to the Internet. They will therefore very likely remain a federation of domains, each with its control facilities.

For now, network operators use the control plane mainly for internal use, such as traffic engineering, for example to improve the QoS of regular IP traffic.

Finally, time is not managed by the control plane and planning must be done in the management plane. Several solutions have been deployed in grids to enable users or grid managers to directly access the control functions of the optical network to dynamically provision very-high-speed links and solve their bulk-transfer problems.

Chapter 8

Bandwidth on Demand

In this chapter, we explore a new type of service that is starting to be commercialized and has very interesting advantages in the context of computing networks. Such a service can be invoked either for database-transfer operations during the computation's initialization phase (*stage-in*) or for an entire session duration, particularly to ensure fluid access to the remotely stored data.

In this chapter, the term service can be taken in the economic sense (a non-material good) or in the sense of the implementation pattern used to provide it. The network services traditionally offered by Internet service providers, e.g. xDSL, consist of providing an access link with a maximum throughput, without guaranteeing that the throughput can be achieved towards a given destination. A circuit with guaranteed throughput between two network destinations is another type of service with a different specification.

Transport networks and their functional planes can be used to provide on-demand network services to users. While the business models for traditional Internet accesses are relatively well-defined, they still need to be established for providing guaranteed resources on demand in a service-oriented model. This business model is not clear yet, even though several approaches have been explored. Another problem associated with the business model is the inter-domain context, because it requires clarification of the relations between participants (users and domains). In a finite world where resources have finite capacities, defining this business model means defining resource sharing and defining who can legitimately access a given quantity of resources.

For years, the tendency has been to find out how to expose services based on this control plane, i.e. to add a service plane to the functional model. The benefit of such guaranteed services has been discussed from the perspective of the user's quality of service (QoS), especially in *grid-computing* communities [JUK 07, DEL 06].

In the next three sections, we present the different services that have been proposed to provide bandwidth: the Internet model, called *network neutrality* because it is its guiding principle, the peer model that, like the GMPLS service model, exposes a lot of information to customers; and the overlay model, where clients access a limited quantity of information. Finally, we will study models based on markets where providers and clients publish their bids and requests, and where a third entity – the market maker – carries out the operation.

8.1. Current service model: network neutrality

The current service model for high-speed Internet access is mainly based on fixed-price billing. Customers pay for an access link with a given maximum capacity, whether they use it or not. The throughput, descending or ascending, that their streams will have is not guaranteed and is determined by many parameters. The principle of network neutrality defines what must and must not be done with user traffic.

There is no single definition of the principle of network neutrality, but all of the definitions assert that all Internet traffic should be dealt with in the same way. The question of finding out whether this principle must always be applied in order to support innovation on the Internet, nuanced in order to provide QoS, or abandoned to favor the provider's profits, is actively debated.

According to this principle, streams obtain resources depending on global mechanisms such as Transport Control Protocol's (TCP's) congestion control and the queue-management algorithm of Internet Protocol (IP) routers. Some hold that packets must be processed based on the *first come, first served* principle to satisfy the principle of network neutrality. In this model, QoS for users (absence of loss, absence of severe congestion, bandwidth) is obtained by overprovisioning the core infrastructure.

The next section presents the architecture or ecosystem of the Internet's current model, focusing on the agents and how they accept traffic from other agents. The limitations of this model are then reviewed.

8.1.1. *Structure*

This ecosystem is made up of customers (C) or users, *access providers* (APs), *transit providers* (TPs), and content providers (CPs). The distinction can be made between business and home in customers' groups to push the analysis further [DHA 08b, XIA 08]. An example of this type of ecosystem is presented in Figure 8.1.

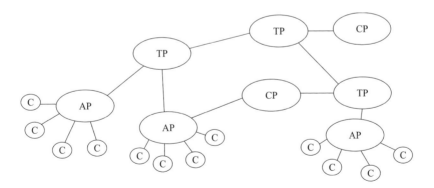

Figure 8.1. *Network-neutrality ecosystem: customers, access providers, transit providers, content providers*

Customers mainly access the content provided by CPs. APs are connected to customers and must negotiate connections to content in order to attract users.

The interconnections of the networks mentioned above are done in Internet eXchange Points (IXP) [AWD 98]. There are two types of relationships between providers: *peering* and *transit*. Whereas the peering relation involves a reciprocal access to each other's contacts, the transit relation provides unilateral access against remuneration. These are business decisions and, as such, based on immediate or expected profitability [BAA 99, CHA 06]. It must be noted that Border Gateway Protocol the inter-domain routing protocol used in the Internet, is particularly well adapted to the implementation of such contracts. By not announcing its routes to neighboring domains, it prevents them from using a given domain for transit because they do not know how to reach their destination via this domain.

As a consequence, the global structure of the Internet is made up of domains (*autonomous systems*) interconnected differently depending on the type of provider they belong to [MAG 01]. Access networks are connected to customers but have an asymmetric need for bandwidth from the other providers since their customers receive more data or content than they send. User traffic is mainly directed to CPs, who might not be directly accessible to the AP. In this case, the AP must buy a transit agreement from a TP. The AP can also convince the CP to establish a direct connection. The customers of TPs are APs and CPs, with the former wanting to reach the latter. CPs also wish to be reachable in order to increase their visibility.

8.1.2. *Limits and problems*

Ensuring network neutrality by processing all traffic in the same way would prevent any improvement in the QoS of a part of traffic. Network neutrality is supposed to offer fair processing of traffic that is the same for everyone. Since different streams can have different needs, this would penalize applications with greater needs, such as high-definition video-conferencing. This is why, depending on the utility obtained for a given value of a QoS parameter (e.g. bandwidth) and the purpose this flow serves, a fair throughput allocation can in fact result in an unfair allocation of actual user utility. As all kinds of utilities can be imagined and they vary depending on clients, this debate is endless and pointless: a system that is fair according to one parameter will be unfair according to another. This is also the case for social welfare.

This is why [DHA 08a] re-focus the debate on the question of profitability for Internet APs. They propose a study of this profitability, under the assumptions of heavy-tail traffic distribution, strong popularity of CPs, and different pricing models considered to be network neutral as they are not based on the content's source. These schemes: charge heavy consumers; limit volume for heavy consumers; or charge CPs.

[DHA 08a] conclude two things from their quantitative study: first, that strategies based on charging are rarely profitable or are highly sensitive to factors over which the AP does not have control; second, that direct peering with major CPs can be profitable, even if it does not respect network neutrality.

8.1.3. *Conclusion*

In this model, the bandwidth provided by adding new fibers or by implementing a new optical circuit is not directly offered to users, but to the network. Bandwidth is then redistributed among flows by the sharing mechanisms of the TCP/IP protocol suite.

To conclude this section, we refer to [CRO 07], which attempts to list the different aspects of the issues related to network neutrality. It concludes that the latter never existed and that it must remain an ideal and not a static constraint limiting innovation.

Following this overview of the current service models and how bandwidth is provided to the user, we move on to the models for network services on demand: *peer* and *overlay* models for bandwidth-delivery services; and market-based models.

8.2. Peer model for bandwidth-delivery services

In the *peer* model, resource descriptions are communicated to users. They can include the fibers and the internal network elements, like routers or switches, or can be made of abstract services that can be composed by users.

Those users can then decide what they will use, depending on their needs and the resource availability published by the network owner. Then, they inform the network of the resources they will use.

In the following sections, we present a few of the projects and propositions revolving around this model. Some are new architectural elements providing functions that can be grouped in a new functional plane (the *services plane*); some are infrastructures, experimental platforms or research projects.

8.2.1. *UCLP/Ca*net*

User Controlled LightPath (UCLP) [WU 02] is a solution to configure, partition and expose the light paths and elements of a physical network. It manipulates light paths like objects and enables users to create their own topologies. This solution was suggested for Ca*net, the Canadian National Research and Education Network (NREN). UCLP has since been developed as a commercial product under the name Argia. Manticore extends this model to layer 3 and provides IP slices.

8.2.2. *GLIF*

In addition to being an organization encouraging the use of optical networks for scientific applications and proposing technical solutions via its work groups, GLIF (*Global Lambda Integrated Facility*) is a federation of optical-network owners that propose optical interconnections for research and e-science. The topology of this network is composed of exchange points, the GOLE (GLIF Open Lightpath Exchanges) interconnected by lambdas. Since this topology is public (see Figure 8.2), and a connection across this network can be requested, GLIF falls in the *peer* models for bandwidth on demand group.

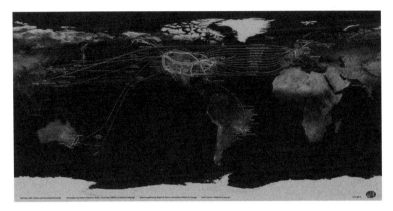

Figure 8.2. *Exchange points and GLIF lambdas (source www.glif.is)*

8.2.3. *Service-oriented* **peer** *model*

The *peer* model was also studied with a service-oriented architecture.

Service Oriented ASTN (SO-ASTN) [BAR 05] is the proposition of a service plane on top of the automatic switched transport networks architecture. Its applications-oriented interface proposes to query information like delay, dit error ratio or the usable or available bandwidth of a set of resources corresponding to the virtual topology requested.

Similarly, [VER 07] proposes a service-oriented architecture where domains publish the services they propose in a directory. Users choose which service corresponds to their needs and invoke it.

8.2.4. *Conclusion*

In this *peer* model, descriptions and information on resources are made available to the user, who can choose those he wishes to use before requesting them from the broker. In this model, the service is composed of users with the knowledge of what can be offered by the provider. This leads to privacy problems. Whereas this model is adapted to National Research and Education Networks (NRENs), network providers today still raise objections. It is worth noting that GEANT2, which links European NRENs, proposes a provisioning service that uses the overlay model via AutoBAHN (*Automated Bandwidth Allocation across Heterogeneous Networks*) [CAM 06].

8.3. Overlay model for bandwidth-providing services

Another model for resource reservation is possible. In this model, users specify their constraints and insert them into requests that they send to a broker. Depending on resource availability, the policies and the constraints expressed by the user, the broker will assign resources to serve the request.

In this model, it is not necessary to provide other information on what is available or not. Like in the public switched telephone work, when a user calls someone he implicitly sends a request for a voice circuit between two points in the network. If the network has enough resources and the receiver is available, the call is carried out and resources are devoted to it. Otherwise, the call is simply rejected. The establishment of rented connection lines is done in a similar fashion, except that it involves manual operations.

8.3.1. *GNS-WSI*

Grid Network Service – Web Services Interface (GNS-WSI) is an interface that has been proposed to perform bandwidth reservation in networks. With this interface, users can request end-to-end paths in advance. The underlying network is abstracted as a cloud. This interface can be used: between customers and *resource managers* (the resources belong to them), or between customers and *resource coordinators* (the resources do not belong to them, but they sell those they obtain from resource managers or other resource coordinators, using the same interface). Figure 8.3 shows this stacking via the interfaces represented by arrows.

This interface was proposed by G-Lambda [WEB 08], a research project carried out at the *National Institute of Advanced Industrial Science and Technology*, KDDI R&D Laboratories, NTT, and the *National Institute of Information and Communications Technology*.

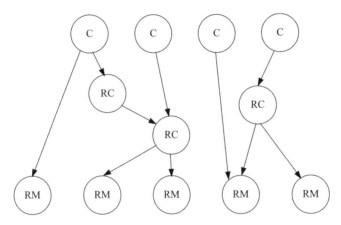

Figure 8.3. *Links between clients, resource coordinators and resource managers*

8.3.2. *Carriocas*

In the Carriocas project (*Distributed Computing over Ultra High Optical Internet Network*) [AUD 07, VIC 09b], the *scheduling and reconfiguration service* accepts requests from clients, which can be higher-order service providers, and serves them using its internal representation of the network and computing resources. The service assumes network resources are provided by a network operator as a connection service described by end points and capacities. Similarly, computing resources are published in the scheduling and reconfiguration service by their owner.

8.3.3. *StarPlane*

The StarPlane project enables the dynamic configuration of the optical network supporting DAS-3, the Dutch grid. The network control plane is based on DRAC (Dynamic Resource Allocation Controller). This interface provides both information about the availability of resources and the means to reserve them. The *StarPlane Management Plane* [GRO 09] provides applications with an interface that enables constraints to be specified on the feasible abstracted services.

8.3.4. *Phosphorus*

European project Phosphorus proposes a service plane for grids that manages both the computing resources and the network – the *Network Service Plane* – which receives requests from grid middleware. Based on the knowledge it has, this service plane determines an end-to-end path across domains [FIG 07]. This service plane is connected, to the south, to *network resource provisioning systems* such as UCLP, DRAC or ARGON (Allocation and Reservation in Grid-enabled Optic Networks). In this context, *Grid-GMPLS* (G^2MPLS) [CIU 08], an extension of GMPLS, has been proposed to act as a control plane taking computing resources into account.

8.3.5. *DRAGON*

The *Dynamic Resource Allocation via GMPLS Optical Networks* (DRAGON) project aims to develop the technologies required to perform dynamic and in-advance reservations of network resources in a heterogeneous and multi-domain network. The domains show an abstract version of their internal topology to other domains. DRAGON provides advance circuit reservation, carried out from a client-side application programming interface. This application programming interface communicates with the *application specific topology builder*, which finds the resources adapted to this request. DRAGON can manage multi-domain networks. Each network has its own *network aware resource broker* that can exchange routing and signaling information with other domains.

8.3.6. *Conclusion*

In the *overlay* model, no information is provided to users apart from the information they obtain when notified their request has been accepted, which cannot be avoided. Nevertheless, the information must be exchanged between domains in the case of a multi-domain request, if this is implemented by a chain model where each domain forwards requests to the next one for validation (see Figure 8.4a).

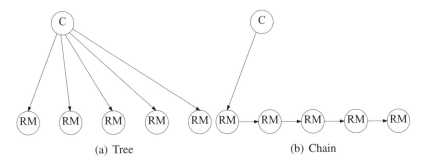

(a) Tree   (b) Chain

Figure 8.4. *The tree- and chain-models for reservation*

If a multi-domain is implemented using the *tree model*, domain composition can be done by a third entity having a customer/provider relation with both domains. This requires a minimum amount of topological information, such as the domain's peering points. If the customers know the resource managers, it is a possible alternative, as shown in Figure 8.4b.

8.4. Bandwidth market

In the two sections above, we saw two different models. One in which users choose the resources they want to use, and one in which the network provider chooses resources based on user constraints. There is a third solution for resource allocation: a commodity market where both sides announce their buying and selling bids [CHE 01].

In these commodity markets, sellers propose bandwidth at a given price (*ask*), buyers request it at another price (*bid*), and the *market maker* carries out the operations. Different types of auctions are possible, but *double auctions* are usually used: buyers and sellers propose a price and a description of the goods; then the *market maker* sets a price so that the market is cleared of the transactions that can be made given each proposal. All the sellers that have requested less than this price sell to all buyers have that offered more.

A *commodity market* implies that bandwidth has been transformed into a commodity, by defining standardized contracts to describe offers in order to have a liquid market in which goods are not too specific and adapted to precise situations [FUS 02]. When the commodity is a segment (a point-to-point connection), its source and destination must be specified, as well as its QoS attributes, the duration of the "reservation" and the date at which it will begin.

Segments can be combined and possibly re-sold, enabling arbitrage if the equivalent paths do not all have the same *spot price*. The possibility of combining segments and buying a set (a path) led Jain and Varaiya [JAI 05] to suggest combinatorial double auctions with an integer linear program to realize the operations.

Advance bandwidth reservation can be seen as a derivative of the commodity as a futures contract. Other derivatives, such as options, could also be used. This market would require risk transfer, hedging and speculation on future bandwidth needs or shortages between certain exchange points. All this would make the bandwidth's *spot price* comparable to that of petrol or cotton, in that it would vary depending on supply/demand and speculation.

Bandwidth is similar to energy in that it is not a storable good. At the beginning of the 2000s, however, some petrol companies like

Enron, had created a bandwidth market. This market failed to mature and disappeared with Enron. The reasons for this failure are not clear, but some explanations proposed include the relatively low price of bandwidth, as well as the technical difficulties in providing bandwidth on demand at the beginning of the 2000s.

8.5. Conclusion

The increase in demand from some users has led network operators affirm that the current Internet model is not viable. In addition to this, with the current model not being in a position to provide guaranteed bandwidth to users who want to pay for this service, new sharing models are being studied or have been deployed in specific contexts (e.g. NRENs). These reservation models fall into three categories, depending on whether the allocation decisions are taken by customers, resource managers or coordinators/*market makers*. All the models presented are focused on bandwidth requests, even if the Phosphorous deliverable mentions that malleable requests can also be proposed in the interface. In the *mechanism design* theory, two typical solutions to the problem of resource allocation exist [HUR 06]: *parameter transfer* (the client submits a request to the operator or the operator exposes the availability of its resources to users); and *direct revelation* (client and operator give details of their parameters to a third agent). It is likely that network operators will favor solutions where they do not need to provide any information.

Optical networks provide a huge amount of bandwidth. The switching paradigm currently used is optical circuit switching, and requires configuration and control. To do this, the functions required for manipulating a network have been grouped into different functional planes.

Unified control planes such as GMPLS offer a set of functions to control these networks and establish circuits for different technologies. In addition to this, management planes enable the management of configuration-, supervision- and performance-related functions. These technologies have been designed for the operator itself.

For some time now, however, research and network communities have been trying to provide users with provisioning on demand. Different approaches have been studied for different contexts: NRENs, private networks, telcos and the Internet.

Among them, the service-on-demand approach for bandwidth delivery establishes a clear interface between customer and provider, where the former expresses his constraints in a request addressed to the latter. If it is accepted, this specification acts as a contract, like a *service level agreement*. These solutions are of interest to users because they move the risk of blocking, which exists for each packet in a packet network, of the reservation procedure. With this method, and provided that the request is not rejected, users could plan their network use and get the resources they need to accomplish their tasks as planned.

For now, network neutrality is the dominant model and bandwidth allocation is determined by: the TCP/IP protocol suite; TCP's control and congestion algorithms; losses and arrivals; and departures of users.

The service provided is the right to use the access links provided by the network operator, but it is not based on the bandwidth obtained by one flow in particular. There is no agreement between the user and the network provider regarding bandwidth allocation because the latter only manages the network's capacity and not the exact way in which it is shared. In this context, the user cannot predict performance. Predictability is important when the network is not the only resource used. For example, if the network is used to interconnect different sites for video-conferencing, in the absence of sufficient network performance the conference is affected. If a dataset has not reached the machine where it is supposed to be processed at the time the reservation starts, there is a waste of CPU time or money.

Chapter 9

Security of Computing Networks

This chapter focuses on the requirements of network security in distributed systems, by taking an example from among the most demanding areas: medical applications. It then reviews the techniques encountered in traditional grid systems and explains how they correspond or not to needs.

9.1. Introductory example

The medical imagery community is confronted with several challenges that make it one of the most constrained communities for distributed infrastructures [VIC 09a]:

– the quantity of data to process, which is several dozens of terabytes annually;

– the distribution of data sources over territories;

– the heterogeneity of data to be processed;

– the confidentiality of medical data, which is necessary for preserving the privacy of patients.

Security demands are important and must imperatively be addressed by the solutions implemented in the systems in order for distributed computing to be accepted by the medical community. All the data for which confidentiality must be preserved belong to patients. Strict rules for the protection of personal medical information must be followed, particularly when the data are transported from acquisition sources to remote processing and storage sites. The development of *secure communication channels* is indispensable. Nevertheless it is not enough to guarantee the protection of the stored data and associated metadata. For example, a file's name usually carries significant information by itself, and possibly even extra information that may be sensitive. The process of data analysis applied is sensitive in itself, because it characterizes the nature of the pathology that affects the patient. Many scientific studies of medical data are carried out from sets of anonymized data, and on local resources only, in order to apply these constraints that are strongly delimited by law. Despite such a need for data privacy, the use of new data is important for clinical applications and can even be an obligation imposed by clinical ethical committees. The potential advantages for a patient whose data are used in a scientific study should actually always be applicable to this person.

It is not acceptable, for a clinical institution, that the access to its data resources should be managed externally by a centralized organization. *Access control* policies must ensure that each organization can control its own medical data and no other organization's data. The access-control technique must enable the implementation of fast access-control rules in the context of medical studies whose lifespan is short (typically a few weeks), as well as the composition of very dynamic groups (such as the small groups of specialists involved in each study). Despite these strong constraints, computing grids were identified as an important tool for supporting various biomedical research activities, including the processing of: large medical databases; large-scale epidemiology studies; statistical population studies; medical simulation; and research on rare diseases.

To summarize, medical applications require the distributed computing environment to guarantee data protection and confidentiality as well as adaptable and dynamic access control:

(1) *ensuring data protection*: data are not accessible to any stranger even if the execution infrastructures can physically extend to multiple organizations. In particular, data must not be exposed during transfer or during the storage on disk;

(2) *confidentiality* to ensure that no external, unauthorized person is capable of following the data stream or the computations applied to the data of any patient in particular. It is also necessary to ensure that no-one from the outside can access the data;

(3) *dynamic and adaptable access control* to enable a entirely personalized and clearly defined context.

In the next section we explain how security layers existing in the current production grids partially cover data- and resource-protection needs, and then show their limits and present a few new techniques based in particular on infrastructure-virtualization techniques.

9.2. Principles and methods

Grid infrastructures allow the large-scale alliance of communities of users and their institutional resources. The resources considered are hardware processing and storage resources as well as scientific data, computing procedures or data-analysis algorithms. One of the main obligations of the middleware is therefore to precisely control the way in which the resources used are shared: access control, delegation and enforcement of policies on a large scale – even sometimes at a global level.

The main security needs in a grid are:

– user authentication;

– authorization of access to distributed resources;

– integrity of the data and codes stored and moved;

– confidentiality of the data and codes stored and moved;

– non-repudiation.

Ten years ago, it was acknowledged that Internet technologies only brought partial answers to these questions. The Internet architecture manages the communication and exchange of information between computers but does not provide integrated approaches for the coordinated use of resources over several sites. As a result, specific security solutions were deployed that supported rights and policies management when computations extend to several institutions, as well as resource- and service-management protocols that secured the remote accesses to computing resources and data.

9.2.1. *Security principles*

Below we restate the security principle set out in [SAL 75] that must guide the design of any security system:

– Economy of mechanism: the security system must be as simple and as small as possible. *One single well-locked access must be enough to protect the treasure hidden in the safe.*

– Fail-safe default: by default, permissions are not granted. Authorization is given explicitly and as nominatively as possible. *The door is automatically closed. It is only opened to those who are invited.*

– Separation of privileges: when possible, install a protection mechanism that requires two different keys to unlock. This method is more robust than the one that allows access with a single key. *Preferably, two different locks will be put in.*

– Least privilege: every program and every user of the system must be able to operate by using the smallest set of privileges possible to complete the job.

– Least common mechanism: minimize the number of mechanisms that are common to more than one user.

– Psychological acceptability: it is essential that the man-machine interface be designed to facilitate usage, so that users regularly and automatically apply the protection mechanism correctly. *An unused security system is useless. It is useless to put in a lock if the door of the safe is always left open.*

9.2.2. *Controlling access to a resource*

The sharing of distributed resources within a multi-domain environment raises complex security-policy questions, at the core of which is the capacity to make an *authorization decision* when a shared resource is accessed. The fundamental question that is posed each time a resource is invoked is: "does this user (or his program) have the permission to access this resource?"

In traditional grid security systems, the first resource the user accesses authenticates him using his certificate provided by a public key infrastructure (PKI). This resource, through a trusted third party, controls the association of the public key provided and provides a user identifier (for example a connection name or a unique Lightweight Directory Access Protocol name). Resources can then consult (directly or indirectly through another entity) *access control list* (ACL) bases that indicate the permissions associated with this user. Authorization is then granted or witheld, depending on this ACL. Figure 9.1, taken from [FOS 98], is a diagram of the main steps necessary for authorizing access to a grid resource.

Security solutions for grid services [FOS 98] are generally based on the combination of a *Global PKI* for the network environment and one ACL per resource. The resource proceeds to user *authentication* on the basis of the authentication certificate provided by the user and makes an *authorization* decision based on the ACL of the resource and the identity of the user (for example a connection name or the *distinguished name*).

In grids, communities of users are identified as *virtual organizations* (VOs) that group together users and computer resources from the same establishment and collaborate in the context of a common objective. Technically, VOs are implemented in grid infrastructures using the security layer that is the very basis of grid middleware. The implementation of VOs necessitates at least user authentication.

The most widespread grid security infrastructure is *Grid Security Infrastructure* or GSI, the security infrastructure of the Globus system

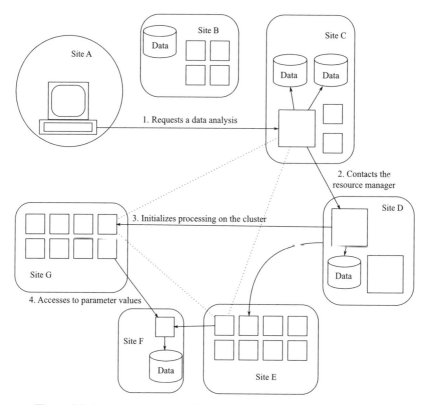

Figure 9.1. *Steps necessary to authorize access to a grid resource [FOS 98]*

that is an extension of the X509-certificate standard based on PKI security.

The GSI generates certificates that conform to the X.509 standard and include four primary parts:

– the name of the subject representing the certificate;

– the public key of the subject;

– the identity of the certification authority (CA) that signs the certificate;

– the signature of the CA.

This model was widely used in grid infrastructures, including the very-large-scale European grid (Enabling Grids for EsciencE or EGEE)[1] and the American Open Science Grid[2].

The GSI offers fundamental security functionalities, such as user authentication and encryption of the transferred data. The authentication functionality is used to control the access to resources.

When the grid paradigm was first explored, the emphasis was placed on the large-scale sharing of computing resources. Access control was developed at a very crude level. The minimum requirement to access resources via GSI requires a user to possess a valid user certificate that was issued by a known CA. Consequently, network access is controlled by the high-level organization, with a CA generally being used at a national level. Nevertheless, network access must often be controlled at a smaller scale, and complementary access-control services have been provided. For example, in the EGEE grid, VO-management servers were introduced with the aim of providing per-VO access-control management. Each server manages VOs independently via a local VO administrator.

Users can also be linked to different roles and groups within the same VO. However, few grid services currently available take into consideration the granularity of groups and roles.

9.2.3. *Limits of the authentication approach*

The traditional authentication approach has drawbacks in terms of evolutivity regarding the number of participating domains. In particular, the load necessary for reconfiguring the shared environment (for example, adding or dropping a resource, a user or an organization) is rather high compared to the envisioned dynamic resource sharing. Although it can be legitimate to require user authentication at the

---

1. www.eu-egee.org.
2. www.opensciencegrid.org.

level of a local site, authentication at the resource-sharing level is not necessary in itself in order to make an authorization decision.

A major inconvenience of the *authentication* approach is that it often requires a global PKI, which requires that all of the grid's entities trust all the CAs of the security domains that make up the grid. Consequently, if one of the domains is compromised, the entire grid can be compromised, rather than just the elements in direct relation with the compromised node. The flexibility of these grids is also affected by the fact that adding or dropping a domain from the grid generates enormous administrative overheads. In other words, when the size of the grid environment increases, its global properties of robustness, flexibility and security decrease, which severely limits the evolutivity of these environments.

9.2.4. *Authentication versus authorization*

Looking at the authorization problems that have contributed to the implementation of security solutions in distributed networks and systems, it appears that there are many examples where these problems have been solved by an *authorization-centered approach* [IOA 00, NIK 99, NIK 03] rather than by an *authentication-centered approach*.

All these solutions are built around a distributed security-infrastructure model like *Simple PKI* or SPKI [ELL 99]. These models are based on the assumption that when a security decision must be taken, authentication is not necessary in itself, but it is, above all, authorization that matters. When an entity exposes a resource and makes it accessible to other users, it is more interested in verifying that an entity (e.g. a user or a group) is authorized to access this resource rather than knowing what its name is. In addition, knowledge of the entity's name is, in general, insufficient to make the authorization decision. It is often necessary to examine an ACL defining *what this entity is authorized to do*. The ACL associates a *name* with particular *rights* (*authorization*, *capacity* or *permission*).

For example, in a distributed implementation of a firewall [IOA 00], the firewall needs to know whether a particular packet is authorized to cross it. If the authorization decision process relies on authentication, clearly knowing the name of the packet's sender (e.g. Bob Smith) is not sufficient to make the authorization decision. The firewall must also be configured to search an ACL for the definition of what this sender is authorized to do (e.g. send only Transport Control Protocol [TCP] packets with port number 80 as a destination through this firewall).

In the *authorization* approach, the name of the entity required is the public key only. The true name (for example Bob Smith, Foo Company) is not used for decision-making when an entity attempts to access a resource. Therefore, when the entity initiates a transaction to the resource, it sends its public key and signs the message with a chain of certificates. This certificate chain is made up of multiple ordered authorization certificates, each of them delivered by a public key (the sender) to another public key (the subject) and granting specific permissions (e.g. a `rwxr-xr-x` file permissions mask or an `operator.reboot .*` privilege). To grant authorization, the resource controller must examine such a certificate chain from the resource controller's public key up to the public key of the entity accessing the resource. The subject and the sender of each intermediate certificate must, respectively, be the sender of the next certificate in the chain or the subject of the previous certificate in the chain. The intersection of the permissions granted by the certificates in the chain must be a superset of the permissions required by the access policy of the resource.

9.2.5. *Decentralized approaches*

Taking into consideration the recent innovations in operating systems and IP technologies, a decentralized and distributed approach to security for grid multi-domain environments has been proposed in [LAG 05]. The argument put forward is that limited evolutivity of existing solutions is not inherent to problems that have to be solved, but rather a consequence of the *a priori* choice of a technology, namely, authentificating users on the global scale at the point of access, and sharing of resources. The basic idea of this alternative approach relies on the fact that systematic user authentification is not necessary in itself for taking an authorization decision at the level of the shared resource. The approach proposed reuses and combines basic security blocks that enable a totally distributed security architecture to be constructed. These blocks are network virtualization, Host Identity Protocol (HIP), authorization delegation and certificates provided by Simple Public Key Infrastructure.

9.3. Communication security

Beside access control, channel protection is also critical in distributed environments. A grid environment must provide the same three fundamental services as a computer: computing, storage and communication. While network communication is, in a way, an add-on to the regular personal computer, it is important to understand that the situation is very different with a distributed system like the grid: the communication channels constitute the backbone of the grid because the geographically distributed computing and storage units cannot collaborate without communicating with each other.

Consequently, and because of the core security principles set out above, secure communication channels must be the foundations on which a secure grid is built. In addition to this, these secure communication channels should be available in an environment where:

– the relations between grid entities – for example users, services, resources, organizations, etc. – are dynamic and can have a short duration;

– the network's interconnection can increase, decrease, move, etc. It is not a fixed entity regarding location and composition;

– the entities should be able to use the communication infrastructure in a transparent way: the end user, applications, tools and application programming interfaces behave as if they were using an ordinary TCP/IP network, be it the Internet or an intranet.

The deployment and management of secure communication channels between very dynamic node coalitions must be carried out by the communicating end points themselves because they have a better view of what the user and the application need in terms of communication security.

To ensure communication security, several solutions of physical or virtual private networks have been proposed and deployed in grids. Below, we list the different approaches that are based on the OSI model and inherit the advantages and drawbacks from the corresponding layer of abstraction:

– *securing at the session level*. Securing at the session level is very much used in the Internet. It involves techniques such as SSL and SSH. It is very close to the user but requires explicit management from the programmer;

– *securing at the transport level*. Securing at the transport level is done mainly across the TLS layer. This level offers more transparency to the user. Security in Globus and the derived middleware (gLite of the EGEE) happens at this level;

– *securing at the network level*. It is possible to create virtual private networks and establish secure communications at the network-layer level. It is done with either IP encapsulation within IP or with the IPsec protocol.

We do not detail these different security technologies, which are common in the Internet. The interested reader can refer to specialized books on Internet security.

9.4. Network virtualization and security

Virtualization turned out to be a very useful mechanism for solving various security and administration problems for sharing a computing or network resource between several entities or administrative domains.

9.4.1. *Classic network-virtualization approaches*

Network virtualization exists both at the layer-2 (the link layer) and layer-3 (network layer) levels of the Open Systems Interconnection reference model:

– the *IEEE 802.1Q Virtual Local Area Network (VLAN) standard* is an example of layer-2 virtualization: VLANs are multiple logical instances that can coexist on the same physical local network;

– the *IPsec standard* is an example of layer-3 virtualization: an IPsec tunnel (with encapsulation within ESP (Encapsulating Security Payload) or AH (Authentication Header)) gives the illusion of a secure point-to-point connection, while packets effectively travel using a multi-hop protocol on an insecure path.

These two solutions also provide access-control functionalities. A VLAN can be configured by port or by network identifier to process, receive, send and forward only the packets labeled with correct VLAN identifiers. This enables different virtual local networks to remain isolated from each other.

An IPsec stack is associated with a *security policy database* that specifies the node's access-control policy, which is similar to a routing table or a firewall except that the input rules are generally indexed by a 5-tuple (the source address, source port, destination address, destination port, protocol number). This policy also specifies what action should be carried out on the packet. For example, besides IPSec processing (encryption and/or protection of integrity), actions can also include packet rerouting or dropping.

Other network-virtualization solutions, based on encapsulations (IP-in-IP tunnel) or the addition of an identifier (multi protocol label switching) also enable traffic and communications to be isolated. This is called L3VPN or L2VPN, depending on the level of abstraction (network layer or datalink layer) considered.

If the communication that needs to be secured occurs between numerous distinct entities belonging to numerous administrative domains, the *point-to-point* VPN model is not a convenient solution because the number of tunnels to manage increases with the square of the number of entities.

New technologies were therefore designed at the level of layers 2 and 3 to enable the management and deployment of the so-called *Provider-Provisioned VPN* (PPVPN), in which a service provider is responsible for managing and deploying a superposition of network meshes between several remote sites. The links of these meshes are point-to-point VPN tunnels.

Nevertheless, VPN management and deployment between very dynamic node coalitions are best solved by the end points themselves (rather than trusted third parties). This is because they have a better view of what the user and the communication applications need. It is possible to use a protocol such as *Host Identity Protocol*, which enables true end-to-end VPN solution.

9.4.2. *The HIP protocol*

In the traditional TCP/IP stack, the IP address plays two independent roles: *location* and *identification*.

The network-level protocols (for example IPv4 and IPv6) use the location role of the IP address to route packets, while the high-level protocols (for example TCP and User Datagram Protocol) use the identification role of an IP address by naming the end points (for example sockets).

This deliberate confusion between these different roles means that high-level layers are dependent on location. These layers break and infringe the end-to-end principle when network mobility and *multi-homing* cause modification of the IP address.

The HIP protocol [MOS 06] proposed by the Internet Engineering Task Force splits up these two roles, while keeping a link between identifiers and locators. It is a virtualization of the network infrastructure from a higher layer. The space of identification names defined by HIP contains the host's public key, which is called a *host identity*.

Since an identifier must sometimes be incorporated in the fixed-size field of an existing protocol or application programming interface, the HIP specification also defines the *host identity tag*, a hash of the public key truncated to 128 bits.

A typical application of this protocol is to no longer directly use IP addresses as identifier, but rather the *host identity* or the *host identity tag*. The HIP layer is in charge of the address's conversion into an appropriate *locator IP*, representing the node's address.

9.5. Conclusion

Security is a very critical aspect of computing networks that includes, on the one hand, access control to distributed and mutualized resources, and on the other hand communication security. The most common solution is the GSI system that uses public-key cryptography and brings:

– a secure communication (authentication and confidentiality);

– a relatively centralized security system;

– *single sign on* with delegation of credentials.

In this chapter, we have shown that addressing security needs can be very demanding. The solutions deployed today in grids do not fully address these needs but enable their robust usage by scientific communities. The extension of network-computing technologies to the industrial world and to the general public requires simpler, more flexible and extensible solutions. Infrastructure virtualization as well as distributed-security approaches are very promising solutions for the dynamic creation of personalized and adaptable trust domains.

Chapter 10

Practical Guide for the Configuration of High-speed Networks

Transporting large volumes of data over long distances requires a hardware and software configuration of the equipment used for sending and receiving as well as an adapted transport protocol. Using parallel flows is a technique often applied by grid users to compensate for parametering difficulties or for the shortcomings of certain hardware configurations.

Furthermore, today high-speed transport protocols with the same fairness and convergence properties as Transport Control Protocol (TCP) are available. For the most part, they are available by default in modern operating systems. They help users to considerably increase performance on Internet links with very high bandwidth-delay products.

Chapter 5 has shown that obtaining optimal performances in a multi-flow context is a technical problem that remains difficult to solve. It is therefore necessary to use diagnostic and calibration tools, such as PATHNIF [GUI 09].

In the following, we provide a few practical tips for choosing the hardware configuration and then adjusting the software configuration to improve communication performance in a very high-speed network.

10.1. Hardware configuration

10.1.1. *Buffer memory*

Buffer memory is designed to temporarily store packets in intermediary equipment throughout their journey along a network path. It is one of the most common and most efficient ways for limiting the impact of traffic bursts and softening the effects of congestion. These buffer memories can be put at the sender and the receiver, as well as at all the network's packet routers and switches.

To get good performance, potentially all the flows carrying out bulk transfers would need to have access to a buffer memory space of the same order of magnitude as their bandwidth-delay product. Indeed, this value corresponds to the maximum quantity of data that can be in transit in the network and has not yet been acknowledged. A smaller quantity in the sending host, for example, does not allow congestion events in the network to be anticipated. A larger quantity is useless. In principle, when the emitter receives a packet acknowledgment, it releases the packet that had been copied in buffer memory for possible retransmission in case of error.

There are also buffer memories in intermediate routers. Over the past few years, numerous studies have tried to determine the ideal size of buffer memory to use in routers. There is no consensus yet on this issue, and the size used by most router vendors remains that of a 100 ms bandwidth-delay product shared by all flows. Nevertheless it would seem that the optimal size is smaller and inversely proportional to the number of flows traversing the router.

10.1.2. *PCI buses*

The PCI (Peripheral Component Interconnect) bus (like its later versions) is a serial local bus that has been used in most computers since the 1990s. The advantage of this architecture is that it enables two peripheral devices connected to it to communicate without having to go through the processor. The PCI bus can become a bottleneck, however, because data must pass at least once through it before being sent by the network card.

Indeed the first version of the PCI-X standard, with its theoretical maximum throughput of 1,066 MB/s, does not allow the optimal use of a 10 Gbit/s card but is more than enough to allow a 1 Gbit/s[1] card to operate at nominal speed. As a comparison, as one PCI-express line (a new high-performance standard evolved from PCI) is able to achieve a full-duplex throughput of 2,000 Mbit/s, a PCI-express card x8 (using eight PCI-express lines) is necessary to be able to make 10 Gbit/s transfers.

10.1.3. *Computing power: CPU*

A few years ago, the equation $1\,\text{GHz} = 1\,\text{Gbit/s}$ was often mentioned to highlight the existence of a bottleneck at the level of the processor, which is used for data processing, packeting and copying the packets multiple times into the right queues. This is less often the case these days because of the systematic use of direct memory access to offload memory-copy operations from the CPU and because of the evolution of CPU frequencies and architectures (the switch to multi-CPU/multi-core architectures). The problem can, however, reappear for 10 Gbit/s interfaces because the number of packets to process per second significantly increases.

One solution to reduce the processor's workload is to increase the size of packets, if this feature is available in the network interface card. In this case, *jumbo-frames* are used. In this instance, it is necessary to make sure that large frames are supported by all the network equipment on the path (path maximum transfer unit). If the processor is composed

---

1. The PCI-X standard had been proposed with the aim of replacing "normal" PCI cards, whose throughput is limited to 1,064 Mbit/s.

of several cores, it also possible to share the load more efficiently between the different cores by using several processes to carry out the transfer task. It is nevertheless necessary to check that packets transmitted and received in parallel are replaced in the correct order.

The processing required by some protocols can be costly, for example in the case of the selective acknowledgment or SACK optimization, which improves the detection of simultaneous multiple losses. When many packets are in flight and non-adjacent losses are observed, the protocol must analyze the complete data structure to find the actual losses.

10.1.4. *Random access memory: RAM*

The speed of access to the random access memory (RAM) also impacts performance. During a network transmission, there are on average four exchanges with the RAM. The current RAM modules have enough bandwidth to handle very high throughputs. For example, for a DDR200 PC1600 module operating at 200 MHz on a 100 MHz bus (FSB), the theoretical maximum throughput is 12.8 Gbit/s. The technique, called *dual channel* (use of RAM modules in identical pairs), allows the RAM's bandwidth to be doubled.

Nevertheless, the RAM is shared by the entire system and it is therefore necessary to correctly dimension this component to prevent it from becoming a bottleneck. Since at least four RAM reads/writes are necessary when routing a packet in the network card, it is necessary to provision five to six times more bandwidth than the network throughput sought.

The ideal RAM size will depend on the volume of data to be sent; it is necessary to have at least the capacity to put all the buffer memory used by TCP into RAM in order to avoid round trips with the disk.

10.1.5. *Disks*

Read and write operations on disks are necessary for moving the data to be processed. A bottleneck can therefore appear at this level. In addition to the limitations related to the type of bus and disk interface (SATA 2,400 Mbit/s, IDE 1,064 Mbit/s, SCSI up to 2,560 Mbit/s), the properties of the hard disk must also be taken into consideration. Typical transfer speeds for modern disks range between 400 Mbit/s and 800 Mbit/s, which is not enough to handle a 1 Gbit/s data stream.

To limit the impact of this parameter, a common technique used is to perform simultaneous parallel writes on multiple disks. This can typically be done using the *redundant array of independent disks* technology. Faster disks can also be used, such as those using the *solid state drive* technology. They also have drawbacks, however, including limited size, high cost, etc. Using a larger memory cache can also contribute to improving performance.

10.2. Importance of the tuning of TCP parameters

This section presents the importance and necessity to tune the TCP parameters in order to obtain satisfying performances in the case of very-high-speed networks. Taking into consideration the overhead caused by TCP, IP and Ethernet headers, the maximum throughput that can be obtained at the application level on a 1 Gbit/s Ethernet link is 941.5 Mbit/s. In grids, however, users who might not be network experts can rarely obtain such performances.

This problem is illustrated in Tables 10.1 and 10.2, taken from [GUI 06]. Table 10.1 corresponds to the matrix of the average application throughput (averaged over 300 s of continuous transfer with *Iperf*) for a single TCP flow between two 1 Gbit/s machines located on different physical sites of the Grid5000[2] platform at the time of its launch in 2005. The experiment was carried out using the default TCP parameters of the GNU/Linux images installed on the different sites. Some sites, such as Orsay or Nancy, had a different initial configuration (especially the size of buffer memory used by TCP, which was greater than the default value of 256 KB used in the GNU/Linux kernel), which

---

2. www.grid5000.org.

explains their better performance. For most site couples, the average application throughput is below 100 Mbit/s, which corresponds to a performance deficit of more than 90%.

		Source								
		Bordeaux	Grenoble	Lille	Lyon	Nancy	Orsay	Rennes	Sophia	Toulouse
Destination	Bordeaux		58,1	61,8	55,9	81,2	111	76,3	68,9	181
	Grenoble	32,3		34,0	151	39,8	33,7	34,3	52,6	48,4
	Lille	53,3	70,0		53,6	112	199	55,0	44,3	33,9
	Lyon	61,5	230	71,2		97,6	106	49,8	100	72,0
	Nancy	48,0	162	78,5	52,4		777	54,7	43,3	32,0
	Orsay	67,8	54,1	150	58,8	936		68,7	36,2	50,8
	Rennes	64,2	33,6	46,6	41,4	45,5	56,5		27,4	26,3
	Sophia	47,0	46,1	29,5	67,4	28,9	22,3	25,1		34,0
	Toulouse	166	47,6	29,8	65,7	29,7	44,3	26,3	36,1	

Table 10.1. *Average throughput matrix for an unadjusted TCP stream between two nodes located in two different sites of Grid5000 at the time the platform was created in 2005. The expected throughput is 941 Mbit/s because each sender has a 1 Gbit/s interface*

Table 10.2 presents the results of the same experiment after having put in a more appropriate value for the buffer memory used by TCP. In our scenario, the value chosen is 4 MB, which is greater than the bandwidth delay product of all the possible network paths (because the maximum round trip time – RTT – on Grid5000 is a bit more than 20 ms). In this case, a clear improvement in the performance of the various flows is observed. The average application throughput on most site couples is greater than 800 Mbit/s, which corresponds to a performance loss of about 15% only.

Consequently, it was possible to modify the default kernel images of the sites in order for all users to be able to benefit from adequate performance without worrying too much about fine-tuning TCP.

10.3. Short practical tuning guide

This section summarizes the elements presented in Chapter 5 and illustrates the different practical steps a user has to follow to correctly configure a path between two end hosts in order to benefit from

		Source								
		Bordeaux	Grenoble	Lille	Lyon	Nancy	Orsay	Rennes	Sophia	Toulouse
Destination	Bordeaux		771	725	862	911	884	852	875	685
	Grenoble	900		701	925	812	893	787	911	647
	Lille	738	838		120	922	848	916	598	579
	Lyon	425	912	786		904	740	864	926	730
	Nancy	725	851	742	865		854	938	931	622
	Orsay	799	866	777	869	936		849	878	523
	Rennes	912	831	787	859	914	912		839	651
	Sophia	901	839	653	543	611	900	321		694
	Toulouse	928	859	784	882	933	923	939	909	

Table 10.2. *Average throughput matrix for a TCP stream between two nodes on two different Grid5000 sites after tuning the configuration*

good performance during the transfer of a large quantity of data on GNU/Linux systems.

10.3.1. *Computing the bandwidth delay product*

The first step consists in trying to identify the values of some characteristics of the path crossed. This can also be a maximum value of these characteristics in order to configure a worse/better case. To compute the bandwidth delay product, estimation of the RTT and of the maximum capacity of the path is needed.

The estimation of the RTT can be done very easily by using the *Ping* utility, which can also collect information on the average loss rate, p, of the path. This tool enables an estimate of the average throughput attainable using a response function to be computed from the transport protocol used (which will give a maximum boundary). However in the case of a network that is not very congested, the loss rates are so low that they are sometimes difficult to measure.

The link's maximum capacity is harder to estimate. A link-capacity detection application like *pathload*[3] can be used. *Pathload* uses the

---

3. See www.cc.gatech.edu/fac/Constantinos.Dovrolis/bw-est/.

spread of a packet train to calculate an estimator. The nominal capacity displayed on the network interface can also be used in to get a worse/better scenario.

10.3.2. *Software configuration*

The two most important parameters are the size of the buffer memory used by TCP and the size of the queue in the network card's driver.

Depending on the position of the end host, it will be necessary to modify the size of buffers: the write buffers for data sending (*tcp_wmem* and *wmem_max*, which are found respectively in /proc/sys/net/ipv4 and /proc/sys/net/core); and the read buffers for data reception (*tcp_rmem* and *rmem_max*).

The *tcp_*mem* are value triplets that correspond to the minimum, the initial and the maximum memory value that can be attributed to a TCP socket. The **mem_max* corresponds to the total memory available for the various open TCP connections. In each case, the max value must be at least equal to the bandwidth delay product.

The other parameter, *txqueuelen*, must be configured using *ifconfig*, the standard GNU/Linux utility for configuring network interfaces. The command line to use looks like this:

```
ifconfig IF txqueuelen VALUE
```

where *IF* is the name of the network interface considered and *VALUE* the value of *txqueulen* to use. This number is computed relative to the maximum size of the congestion window wanted. In the ideal case, it must be possible to place the entire window in the queue, therefore: $VALUE \simeq BDP/1,500$[4].

---

4. 1,500 is the approximate value of an Ethernet packet's maximum size.

It should be noted that it might not be possible to modify this parameter. The ability to modify the parameter will depend on the implementation of the network card's driver.

10.3.3. *Other solutions*

If, after this software configuration phase, the performances obtained are still not satisfactory, it is possible to explore the following options:

– if the RTT or the loss rate, p, is significant, it can be advantageous to use a high-speed TCP variant such as those presented in Chapter 5. This is done by simply changing the value of the *tcp_congestion_control* variable that is found in */proc/sys/net/ipv4/* in order to change the TCP variant that will be used by all TCP connections opened from then on[5];

– the use of several parallel TCP flows can significantly improve the performances, as shown in Chapter 5;

– in order to achieve more significant throughputs, it is also possible to use larger packet sizes (maximum transfer unit), called jumbo-frames, from end-to-end in the intermediary equipment. This has the effect of reducing the headers' overhead and increasing the effective throughput of the network (going from a throughput loss of $52/1,500 = 3.5\%$ per packet to $52/8,192 = 0.6\%$, for example);

– it can also be interesting to study the characteristics of the hardware used in end hosts in order to determine whether there is already a hardware bottleneck. It is not unusual for the PCI bus to be under-dimensioned compared to throughput needs.

PATHNIF[6] explores all these possibilities, helps users to configure end hosts in the best way, and determines where the bottlenecks are located on a network path.

NOTE. It is important to be aware of the impact of adding buffer memory on a network path, especially regarding latency increase.

_____

5. It is only valid if the modules (or the kernel) corresponding to these variants were compiled.

6. See http://ens-lyon.fr/LIP/RESO/Software/PATHNIF/.

This type of operation is necessary to obtain good performance with applications necessitating a significant network throughput (e.g. File Transfer Protocol or FTP, video streaming video), but it can have a negative impact on all of the applications that depend strongly on latency (e.g. voice-over-IP and online games). To solve this type of problem, it is advisable to implement a quality of service policy in order to give greater priority to packets sent by applications penalized by a high latency.

10.4. Use of multi-flow

This section presents an experiment that illustrates the benefit of using parallel flows in order to obtain better performance from the network.

Parallel flows can be used in different ways. Some applications can natively use several parallel flows, such as *Iperf*, the application that was used to carry out the following experiment. This is also the case of most peer-to-peer applications that use a large number of simultaneous connections to carry out a file transfer. The other way consists of using a software library such as PSockets [SIV 00], which transforms the standard calls to the socket library in order to use parallel flows. This does, however, require specific recompiling of the applications concerned.

In this experiment, carried out between the Grid5000 sites of Nancy and Rennes (France), the number of parallel flows used for making simultaneous, one-way transfers between 11 node couples was made to vary. Each node is capable (and configured to this end) of sending at 1 Gbit/s and all of them share a 10 Gbit/s bottleneck. The link has an RTT of about 11 ms. The TCP variant used in this experiment is BIC-TCP. Each flow is started separately (with a one-second interval) in order to avoid interactions during the Slow Start phase.

Figure 10.1 shows the impact of the number of parallel flows on the aggregate average application throughput. It can be noted that, as the number of flows is increased, a smoother and greater aggregate average application throughput is obtained, which represents a better use of the link's capacity.

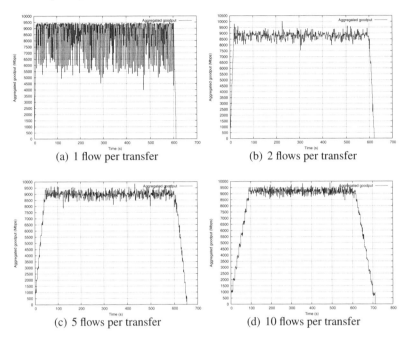

(a) 1 flow per transfer   (b) 2 flows per transfer

(c) 5 flows per transfer   (d) 10 flows per transfer

Figure 10.1. *Example of the impact of the number of parallel flows on the aggregate average application throughput*

Table 10.3 summarizes the results obtained in this experiment. We observe an increase in the application throughput that can go up to 10%. Jain's fairness index [JAI 91] is an index that enables the fair sharing of a resource to be quantified. In the case of this experiment, we notice that the fairness is not impaired by the use of these parallel flows.

NOTE. The use of parallel flows has a strong impact on network sharing between different hosts sharing a link. Indeed, while TCP allows fair bandwidth sharing, this occurs at the flow level. A host that uses a larger number of flows[7] than the others will obtain a larger share of bandwidth

---

7. As long as it does not congest its own access link.

Number of flows per host	1	2	5	10
Total number of flows	11	22	55	110
Aggregate average application throughput (Mbit/s)	8,353.66	8,793.92	8,987.49	9,207.78
Average application throughput per flow (Mbit/s)	761.70	399.83	163.53	83.71
Application throughput gain	—	4.9%	7.3%	9.8%
Jain fairness index per flow	0.9993	0.9979	0.9960	0.9973
Jain fairness index per transfer	0.9993	0.9994	0.9998	0.9998

Table 10.3. *Results of the experiment using multiple parallel flows*

than them. Mechanisms have been proposed – especially at the router level – to try to solve this problem, but are not currently deployed on the Internet.

10.5. Conclusion

In this chapter, we highlighted the hardware and software factors influencing the end-to-end performances obtained by a TCP connection. We provided a brief guide to tuning the configuration parameters, enabling users to improve the performance of their transfers in very-high-speed networks.

Conclusion
From Grids to the Future Internet

Since their invention two decades ago, the Internet and the Web have had a very significant impact on our lives. By enabling us to discover and access information on a global scale, they have enabled the very rapid expansion of a completely new industry and brought a new meaning to the verb to *surf*. Despite this, simply being capable of accessing information, as numerous and diversified as it is, is becoming increasingly insufficient. We would also like to be able to process this information and, progressively, want to exploit it in a cooperative way, in distributed teams. It is this need that has pushed the creation of the grid – an infrastructure that enables us to share capacities, to temporarily integrate new services and resources in and between businesses, and that enables active collaborations in distributed environments belonging to multiple organizations and groups.

Today the massive deployment of optical fibers to homes is on the way to revolutionizing not only the field of telecommunications but also that of computation, and even of the computing sector as a whole. The massive increase in access rates and connectivity will enable the globalization of computer resources and the construction of high-performance or ubiquitous distributed systems that are able to address the increasing computing needs of large scientific applications, and also of many industrial, domestic and entertainment applications.

This book has endeavored to show that these hardware advancements and the evolutions of uses push the software and protocols necessary for network use and coordination of exchanges to their limits. Traditional approaches do not in any way guarantee that the potentially accessible capacity is actually achievable.

For example, we explained that in a simple computing session in a distributed environment, an initiator sends data and control programs to a set of computing resources, waits for the results, iterates this process a certain number of times and finally ends the session. The finer the computing grain, the more significant the *end-to-end transmission* delay becomes until it risks damaging the entire application.

It is also desirable, at the level of computing nodes, to minimize the *processing cost related to transmissions*. The *volume of data transported* by applications in many scientific domains (for example genomics, medical imagery, particle physics and astrophysics) is on the way to reaching the scale of the terabyte. Problems linked mainly to the scale factor, heterogeneity and dynamicity at multiple levels are starting to appear. These problems call for appropriate programming paradigms and control software, as well as efficient and specific communication protocols.

The transportation of massive amounts of data is likely to congest current links (or certain critical points) for very long periods without necessarily guaranteeing an effective and correct transfer of all the data. Certain sessions that are too long can fail and simultaneously prevent the circulation of short and urgent messages. Communications taking place on a computing grid also intensively use *reliable data distribution* and collective-operations mechanisms that we do not know how to efficiently process with traditional point-to-point protocols. This is added to by the instability of the load and availability of the network links used during transfers, which can handicap the job scheduler in charge of determining an efficient job sequence.

We have shown that new challenges must be overcome at the level of communication software and protocols to make these infrastructures efficient. The extreme heterogeneity of performance and reliability of the cloud network must be reconciled with intense data movements, which are critical determinants of an application's performance. Therefore, although grids offer considerable potential through aggregation of resources, good application-execution performance can be hard to obtain in practice because of the inadequacy of the data-transfer protocols and software. The different chapters of this book have detailed the facets of performance, quality of service and communications security in distributed computing environments. They have listed the needs and presented the different solutions that are functional today and will be more widely diffused in the future, such as bandwidth services and performance measurement on-demand.

Indeed, pushed by the needs of *on-demand* access to computing resources, transparent access to data and dynamic composition of distributed services, the grid and its successor – the computing cloud – promise to offer completely innovative means of interacting with our information technology infrastructures, doing business and practicing science. This mutation could represent the latest stage of the migration of computing tasks out of our homes – from our computer rooms to our societies – along with telephone relays, electric generators and other invisible technologies that drive our modern world. Future applications will no longer only use personal computers but a large set of interconnected resources.

This scenario of computing and data grids has attracted a lot of attention from both application scientists and the main companies involved in computing. In addition to the complexity that is inherent to the current powerful end systems, resource-sharing and the transparency of available resources has introduced not only new scientific challenges but also a completely new vision and innovative approaches to the design, construction and use of future communication and information-processing systems.

The grid is a vision that has raised a lot of interest and led to a considerable amount of research and development. While several grids exist today and are used daily, it has, however been recognized that after a decade they are far from being technological platforms that can be used by the general public and are not robust enough to address the needs of every application scenario. In addition to this, it is obvious that programming applications in such systems pose several new and complex challenges.

We have shown that in the future, if network technologies allow, it will be desirable to have the middleware and the network cooperate closely with each other to simplify the programmer's work without the loss of performance. An autonomous grid infrastructure will therefore be capable of self-configuration, self-optimization and self-adaptation to the specific needs of each application. Innovation is needed at the level of the cross-layering software mechanisms and of the associated means of performance measurement and adaptation.

Like the Internet, the domain of the grid has evolved from the needs of science. The Internet was developed to respond to the requirement for a means of communication between large computing centers funded in an amalgamated way. These communication links have enabled the sharing of resources and information between these centers, and also enabled other users to access these resources. *Ad hoc* resource-sharing procedures between original groups has highlighted the need for the standardization of protocols in order to communicate with heterogeneous administrative domains. The first-generation grid technology can be seen as an extension or an application of this framework to create a more generic resource-sharing context.

The research that has been carried out the past few years has revealed that grid technology has been raising new challenges regarding network usage as well as transport protocols and paradigm architecture [BAS 05, MAR 05b, SPI 09]. A large deployment of the grid technology and, now, of cloud technology can modify and influence the design of the future Internet, like all of the other transmission technologies and communication applications.

The diversification of network protocols to adapt to specific needs of delay or throughput-guarantee, as well as the advanced use of optical technology, are the main vectors of inspiration and renewing of network approaches that the computing problem brings to the field of communications. These new protocols and services [AGA 09, SOU 09a, SOU 09b, VIC 05a] associated with security techniques adapted to this type of sensitive context will, without a doubt, have a key role to play in the future Internet, which will undoubtedly host an increasing number of applications and services consuming a lot of processing and storage resources. They will be the true springboard of a new efficient and durable technology of autonomous and transparent services, called *cloud services*.

Bibliography

[ACQ 08] ACQUAAH P., LIU J.-M. and CHAN H. A., "Emission and discard priority scheme for optical burst switched networks", *Journal of Optical Networking*, vol. 7, no. 12, pp. 977–988, OSA, 2008.

[AGA 09] AGAPI A., SOUDAN S., PASIN M., VICAT-BLANC PRIMET P. and KIELMANN T., "Optimizing deadline-driven bulk data transfers in overlay networks", *International Conference of Computer Communication and Networking (ICCCN), Track on Pervasive Computing and Grid Networking (PCGN)*, San Francisco, USA, 2009.

[ALL 03] ALLCOCK W., "GridFTP: protocol extension to FTP for the grid", *Grid Forum Document 20*, April 2003.

[ALT 06] ALTMAN E., BARMAN D., TUFFIN B. and VOJNOVIC M., "Parallel TCP sockets: simple model, throughput and validation", *INFOCOM 2006: Proceedings of the 25th IEEE International Conference on Computer Communications*, pp. 1–12, April 2006.

[AND 95] ANDERSON T. E., CULLER D. E. and PATTERSON D. A., "A case for NOW (networks of workstations)", *IEEE Micro*, vol. 15, no. 1, pp. 54–64, 1995.

[AUD 07] AUDOUIN O., ERASME D., JOUVIN M., LECLERC O., MOUTON C., VICAT-BLANC PRIMET P., RODRIGUES D. and THUAL L., "CARRIOCAS project: an experimental high bit rate optical network for for computing intensive distributed applications", *BroadBand Europe'07*, December 2007.

[AUD 09] AUDOUIN O., BARTH D., GAGNAIRE M., MOUTON C., VICAT-BLANC PRIMET P., RODRIGUES D., THUAL L. and VERCHÈRE D., "CARRIOCAS project: towards converged Internet infrastructures supporting high performance distributed applications", *Journal of Lightwave Technology*, vol. 27, no. 12, pp. 1928–1940, 2009.

[AWD 98] AWDUCHE D. O., AGOGBUA J. and MCMANUS J., "An approach to optimal peering between autonomous systems in the Internet", *IC3N '98: Proceedings of the International Conference on Computer Communications and Networks*, Washington, DC, USA, IEEE Computer Society, p. 346, 1998.

[BAA 99] BAAKE P. and WICHMANN T., "On the economics of Internet peering", *Netnomics*, vol. 1, no. 1, pp. 89–105, Kluwer Academic Publishers, 1999.

[BAN 99] BANGA G., MOGUL J. C. and DRUSCHEL P., "A scalable and explicit event delivery mechanism for UNIX", *USENIX Annual Technical Conference*, pp. 253–265, June 1999.

[BAR 05] BARONCELLI F., MARTINI B., VALCARENGHI L. and CASTOLDI P., "A service oriented network architecture suitable for global grid computing", *Conference on Optical Network Design and Modeling*, pp. 283–293, 2005.

[BAS 05] BASSI A., BECK M., CHANUSSOT F., GELAS J.-P., HARAKALY R., LEFÈVRE L., MOORE T., PLANK J. and VICAT-BLANC PRIMET P., "Active and logistical networking for grid computing: the e-toile architecture", *The International Journal of Future Generation Computer Systems (FGCS) – Grid Computing: Theory, Methods and Applications*, vol. 21, no. 1, pp. 199–208, 2005.

[BOD 95] BODEN N. J., COHEN D., FELDERMAN R. E., KULAWIK A. E., SEITZ C. L., SEIZOVIC J. N. and SU W.-K., "Myrinet: a gigabit-per-second local area network", *IEEE Micro*, vol. 15, no. 1, pp. 29–36, 1995.

[BOL 06a] BOLZE R., CAPPELLO F., CARON E., DAYDÉ M., DESPREZ F., JEANNOT E., JÉGOU Y., LANTERI S., LEDUC J., MELAB N., MORNET G., NAMYST R., PRIMET P., QUETIER B., RICHARD O., TALBI E.-G. and IRENA T., "Grid'5000: a large scale and highly reconfigurable experimental grid testbed", *International Journal of High Performance Computing Applications*, vol. 20, no. 4, pp. 481–494, 2006.

[BOL 06b] BOLZE R., CAPPELLO F., CARON E., DAYDÉ M., DESPREZ F., JEANNOT E., JÉGOU Y., LANTERI S., LEDUC J., MELAB N., MORNET G., NAMYST R., PRIMET P., QUETIER B., RICHARD O., TALBI E.-G. and IRENA T., "Grid'5000: a large scale and highly reconfigurable experimental Grid testbed", *International Journal of High Performance Computing Applications*, vol. 20, no. 4, pp. 481–494, 2006.

[BRA 94] BRAKMO L. S., O'MALLEY S. W. and PETERSON L. L., "TCP vegas: new techniques for congestion detection and avoidance", *SIGCOMM*, pp. 24–35, 1994.

[BRA 97] BRADEN R., ZHANG L., BERSON S., HERZOG S. and JAMIN S., Resource reservation protocol (RSVP) – Version 1 functional specification, RFC 2205 (Proposed Standard), September 1997, Updated by RFCs 2750, 3936, 4495.

[BRI 00] BRIGHTWELL R. and MACCABE A., "Scalability limitations of VIA-based technologies in supporting MPI", *Proceedings of the Fourth MPI Developer's and User's Conference*, March 2000.

[BYR 02] BYROM R. *et al.*, "R-GMA: a relational grid information and monitoring system", *2nd Krakow Grid Workshop*, December, 11–14 2002.

[CAM 06] CAMPANELLA M., KRZYWANIA R., REIJS V. and SEVASTI A., "The bandwidth on demand service for the European research and education networks", *International Conference on Photonics in Switching*, pp. 1–4, October 2006.

[CAP 05] CAPPELLO F., DESPREZ F., DAYDE M., JEANNOT E., JEGOU Y., LANTERI S., MELAB N., NAMYST R., VICAT-BLANC PRIMET P., RICHARD O., CARON E., LEDUC J. and MORNET G., "Grid'5000: a large scale, reconfigurable, controlable and monitorable grid platform", *6th IEEE/ACM International Workshop on Grid Computing*, 2005.

[CHA 06] CHANG H. and JAMIN S., "To peer or not to peer: modeling the evolution of the Internet's AS-level topology", *INFOCOM 2006: Proceedings of the 25th IEEE International Conference on Computer Communications*, April 2006.

[CHE 01] CHELIOTIS G., Structure and Dynamics of Bandwidth Markets, PhD thesis, National Technical University of Athens, November 2001.

[CHE 02] CHERVENAK A., DEELMAN E., FOSTER I., GUY L., IAMNITCHI
A., KESSELMANAND C., HOSCHEK W., RIPEANU M., SCHWARTZKOPF
B., STOCKINGER H., STOCKINGER K. and TIERNEY B., "Giggle: a
framework for constructing scalable replica location services", *SC'2002*,
Baltimore, USA, November 2002.

[CHI 89] CHIU D. and JAIN R., "Analysis of the increase/decrease algorithms
for congestion avoidance in computer networks", *Journal of Computer
Networks and ISDN*, vol. 17, no. 1, pp. 1–14, 1989.

[CIA 00] CIACCIO G. and CHIOLA G., "GAMMA and MPI/GAMMA
on GigabitEthernet", *Proceedings of 7th EuroPVM-MPI Conference*,
Balatonfured, Hungary, September 2000.

[CIU 08] CIULLI N., CARROZZO G., GIORGI G., ZERVAS G., ESCALONA
E., QIN Y., NEJABATI R., SIMEONIDOU D., CALLEGATI F., CAMPI
A., CERRONI W., BELTER B., BINCZEWSKI A., STROINSKI M.,
TZANAKAKI A. and MARKIDIS G., "Architectural approaches for the
integration of the service plane and control plane in optical networks",
Optical Switching and Networking, vol. 5, no. 2-3, pp. 94–106, 2008.

[COL 07] COLLABORATIVE D., User direct access transport APIs (UDAPL),
2007, http://www.datcollaborative.org/udapl.html.

[CRO 07] CROWCROFT J., "Net neutrality: the technical side of the debate:
a white paper", *SIGCOMM Comput. Commun. Rev.*, vol. 37, no. 1,
pp. 49–56, ACM, 2007.

[CZA 01] CZAJKOWSKI K., FITZGERALD S., FOSTER I. and
KESSELMAN C., "Grid information services for distributed resource
sharing", *Proceedings of the 10th IEEE International Symposium on
High-Performance Distributed Computing (HPDC-10)*, IEEE Press,
August 2001.

[DEL 06] DE LEENHEER M., THYSEBAERT P., VOLCKAERT B., DE TURCK
F., DHOEDT B., DEMEESTER P., SIMEONIDOU D., NEJABATI R.,
ZERVAS G., KLONIDIS D. and O'MAHONY M., "A view on
enabling-consumer oriented grids through optical burst switching",
Communications Magazine, IEEE, vol. 44, no. 3, pp. 124–131, 2006.

[DHA 08a] DHAMDHERE A. and DOVROLIS C., "Can ISPs be profitable
without violating "network neutrality"?", *NetEcon'08: Proceedings of the
3rd International Workshop on Economics of Networked Systems*, New
York, USA, ACM, pp. 13–18, 2008.

[DHA 08b] DHAMDHERE A. and DOVROLIS C., "Ten years in the evolution of the Internet ecosystem", *IMC '08: Proceedings of the 8th ACM SIGCOMM Conference on Internet Measurement*, New York, USA, ACM, pp. 183–196, 2008.

[DUB 97] DUBNICKI C., BILAS A., LI K. and PHILBIN J., "Design and implementation of virtual memory-mapped communication on myrinet", *Proceedings of the 11th International Symposium on Parallel Processing (IPPS)*, p. 388, 1997.

[EGE 04] EGEE: ENABLING GRIDS FOR E-SCIENCE, 2004, http://www.eu-egee.org.

[EGE 09] EGEE, e2emonit project website, June 2009, http://www.egee-npm.org/e2emonit.

[EIC 92] VON EICKEN T., CULLER D. E., GOLDSTEIN S. C. and SCHAUSER K. E., "Active messages: a mechanism for integrated communication and computation", *Proceedings of the 19th Int'l Symp. on Computer Architecture*, Gold Coast, Australia, May 1992.

[EIC 95] VON EICKEN T., BASU A., BUCH V. and VOGELS W., "U-net: a user-level network interface for parallel and distributed computing", *15th ACM Symposium on Operating Systems Principles (SOSP)*, pp. 40–53, December 1995.

[ELL 99] ELLISON C. *et al.*, SPKI Certificate Theory, IETF, RFC 2693, September 1999.

[ELL 05] ELLANTI M. N., GORSHE S. S., RAMAN L. G. and GROVER W. D., *Next Generation Transport Networks: Data, Management, and Control Planes*, Springer-Verlag, New York, USA, 2005.

[EUD 01] EU DATAGRID H. P., http://www.eu-datagrid.org, 2001.

[FAR 05] FARREL A. and BRYSKIN I., *GMPLS: Architecture and Applications (The Morgan Kaufmann Series in Networking)*, Morgan Kaufmann Publishers Inc., San Francisco, CA, USA, 2005.

[FAR 06] FARREL A., VASSEUR J.-P. and ASH J., A path computation element (PCE)-based architecture, RFC 4655 (Informational), August 2006.

[FIG 07] FIGUEROLA S., CIULLI N., DE LEENHEER M., DEMCHENKO Y., ZIEGLER W. and BINCZEWSKI A., "PHOSPHORUS: single-step on-demand services across multi-domain networks for e-science", WANG J., CHANG G.-K., ITAYA Y. and ZECH H.(Eds), *Proceedings of SPIE, the International Society for Optical Engineering*, vol. 6784, SPIE, 2007.

[FLO 00] FLOYD S., HANDLEY M., PADHYE J. and WIDMER J., "Equation-based congestion control for unicast applications", *SIGCOMM*, August 2000.

[FLO 03] FLOYD S., HighSpeed TCP for large congestion windows, RFC 3649, December 2003.

[FOR 94] FORUM M. P. I., MPI: A Message-Passing Interface Standard, Report no. UT-CS-94-230, 1994.

[FOS 97] FOSTER I. and KESSELMAN C., "Globus: a metacomputing infrastructure toolkit", *The International Journal of Supercomputer Applications and High Performance Computing*, vol. 11, no. 2, pp. 115–128, 1997.

[FOS 98] FOSTER I., KESSELMAN C., TSUDIK G. and TUECKE S., "A security architecture for computational grids", *Proc. 5th ACM Conference on Computer and Communications Security Conference*, pp. 83–92, 1998.

[FOS 02] FOSTER I., KESSELMAN C., NICK J. and TUECKE S., "The physiology of the grid: an open grid services architecture for distributed systems integration", *Open Grid Service Infrastructure WG, Global Grid Forum*, 2002.

[FOS 04] FOSTER I., *The Grid 2: Blueprint for a New Computing Infrastructure*, Morgan Kaufmann, 2004.

[FUS 02] FUSARO P. C., *Energy Convergence: the Beginning of the Multi-Commodity Market*, John Wiley & Sons, 2002.

[G.602] ITU-T Recommendation G.694.1: Spectral grids for WDM applications: DWDM frequency grid, Report, International Telecommunication Union, June 2002.

[G.800] ITU-T Recommendation G.805: Generic functional architecture of transport networks, Report, International Telecommunication Union, March 2000.

[G.801a] ITU-T Recommendation G.8080: Architecture for the automatically switched optical network (ASON), Report, International Telecommunication Union, November 2001.

[G.801b] ITU-T Recommendation G.872: Architecture of optical transport networks, Report, International Telecommunication Union, November 2001.

[GAB 04] GABRIEL E., FAGG G. E., BOSILCA G., ANGSKUN T., DONGARRA J. J., SQUYRES J. M., SAHAY V., KAMBADUR P., BARRETT B., LUMSDAINE A., CASTAIN R. H., DANIEL D. J., GRAHAM R. L. and WOODALL T. S., "Open MPI: goals, concept, and design of a next generation MPI implementation", *Proceedings of the 11th European PVM/MPI Users' Group Meeting*, Budapest, Hungary, pp. 97–104, September 2004.

[GEO 08] GEOFFRAY P. and HOEFLER T., "Adaptive routing strategies for modern high performance networks", *Proceedings of the 16th Annual IEEE Symposium on High-Performance Interconnects*, August 2008.

[GLA 08] GLATARD T., MONTAGNAT J., LINGRAND D. and PENNEC X., "Flexible and efficient workflow deployement of data-intensive applications on grids with MOTEUR", *International Journal of High Performance Computing and Applications (IJHPCA)*, vol. 22, no. 3, pp. 347–360, 2008.

[GOG 04] GOGLIN B., PRYLLI L. and GLÜCK O., "Optimizations of client's side communications in a distributed file system within a myrinet cluster", *Proceedings of the IEEE Workshop on High-Speed Local Networks (HSLN)*, Tampa, Florida, IEEE Computer Society Press, pp. 726–733, November 2004.

[GOG 08a] GOGLIN B., "Design and implementation of open-MX: high-performance message passing over generic ethernet hardware", *CAC 2008: Workshop on Communication Architecture for Clusters*, Miami, FL, IEEE, April 2008.

[GOG 08b] GOGLIN B., "Improving message passing over ethernet with I/OAT copy offload in Open-MX", *Proceedings of the IEEE International Conference on Cluster Computing*, Tsukuba, Japan, IEEE Computer Society Press, September 2008.

[GRO 09] GROSSO P., MARSAL D., MAASSEN J., BERNIER E., XU L. and DE LAAT C., "Dynamic photonic lightpaths in the StarPlane network", *Future Generation Computer Systems*, vol. 25, no. 2, pp. 132–136, 2009.

[GU 07] GU Y. and GROSSMAN R. L., "UDT: UDP-based data transfer for high-speed wide area networks", *Comput. Networks*, vol. 51, no. 7, pp. 1777–1799, 2007.

[GUI 06] GUILLIER R., HABLOT L., VICAT-BLANC PRIMET P. and SOUDAN S., Evaluation des liens 10 GbE de Grid'5000, Research Report no. 6047, INRIA, 2006.

[GUI 09] GUILLIER R. and VICAT-BLANC PRIMET P., "A tool to diagnose hardware and software bottlenecks on an end to end path", 2009, http://www.ens-lyon.fr/LIP/RESO/Software/PATHNIF/index.html.

[GUS 92] GUSTAVSON D. B., "The scalable coherent interface and related standard projects", *IEEE Micro*, vol. 12, no. 1, pp. 10–22, 1992.

[HAC 02] HACKER T., ATHEY B. and NOBLE B., "The end-to-end performance effects of parallel TCP sockets on a lossy wide-area network", *Proc. 16th IEEE-CS/ACM International Parallel and Distributed Processing Symposium (IPDPS)*, 2002.

[HAN 05] HANEMANN A., BOOTE J. W., BOYD E. L., DURAND J., KUDARIMOTI L., LAPACZ R., SWANY D. M., ZURAWSKI J. and TROCHA S., "PerfSONAR: a service oriented architecture for multi-domain network monitoring", *Proceedings of the 3rd International Conference on Service Oriented Computing*, Springer Verlag, LNCS 3826, pp. 241–254, December 2005.

[HAR 05] HARAKALY R., PRIMET P., BONNASSIEUX F. and GAIDIOZ B., "Probes coordination protocol for network performance measurement in GRID environment", *Scalable Computing: Practice and Experience*, vol. 6, no. 1, pp. 71–80, 2005.

[HUR 06] HURWICZ L. and REITER S., *Designing Economic Mechanisms*, Cambridge University Press, 2006,

[IOA 00] IOANNIDIS S., KEROMYTIS A., BELLOVIN S. and SMITH J., "Implementing a distributed firewall", *Proceedings of the 7th ACM Conference on Computer and Communications Security*, 2000.

[IPE] IPERF H. P., http://dast.nlanr.net/Projects/Iperf.

[JAC 88] JACOBSON V., "Congestion avoidance and control", *SIGCOMM '88: Symposium Proceedings on Communications Architectures and Protocols*, New York, USA, ACM, pp. 314–329, 1988.

[JAI 91] JAIN R., *The Art of Computer Systems Performance Analysis: Techniques for Experimental Design, Measurement, Simulation, and Modeling*, Wiley-Interscience, New York, USA, April 1991.

[JAI 05] JAIN R. and VARAIYA P., "Efficient market mechanisms for network resource allocation", *44th IEEE Conference on Decision and Control*, pp. 1056–1061, December 2005.

[JON 06] JONES R. H., UDPmon project website, June 2006, http://www. hep.man.ac.uk/u/rich/net/index.html.

[JUK 07] JUKAN A. and KARMOUS-EDWARDS G., "Optical control plane for the grid community", *Communications Surveys & Tutorials*, IEEE, vol. 9, no. 3, pp. 30–44, 2007.

[KAT 02] KATABI D., HANDLEY M. and ROHRS C., "Congestion control for high bandwidth-delay product networks", *SIGCOMM Comput. Commun. Rev.*, vol. 32, no. 4, pp. 89–102, ACM, 2002.

[KOM 04] KOMPELLA K. and LANG J., Procedures for modifying the resource reservation protocol (RSVP), RFC 3936 (Best Current Practice), October 2004.

[KOM 05] KOMPELLA K. and REKHTER Y., OSPF extensions in support of generalized multi-protocol label switching (GMPLS), RFC 4203 (Proposed Standard), October 2005.

[LAG 05] LAGANIER J. and VICAT-BLANC PRIMET P., "HIPernet: a decentralized security infrastructure for large scale grid environments", *6th IEEE/ACM International Conference on Grid Computing (GRID 2005)*, Seattle, Washington, USA, pp. 140–147, 2005.

[LAU 98] LAURIA M., PAKIN S. and CHIEN A. A., "Efficient layering for high speed communication: fast messages 2.x", *HPDC*, pp. 10–20, 1998.

[LIU 06] LIU S., BASAR T. and SRIKANT R., "TCP-Illinois: a loss and delay-based congestion control algorithm for high-speed networks", *VALUETOOL*, October 2006.

[LOW 04] LOWEKAMP B. B., TIERNEY B., COTTRELL L., HUGHES-JONES R., KIELMANN T. and SWANY M., A hierarchy of network performance characteristics for grid applications and services, Global Grid Forum Proposed Recommendation, May 2004.

[M.300a] ITU-T Recommendation M.3010: Principles for a telecommunications management network, Report, International Telecommunication Union, February 2000.

[M.300b] ITU-T Recommendation M.3400: TMN management functions, Report, International Telecommunication Union, February 2000.

[MAG 01] MAGONI D. and PANSIOT J. J., "Analysis of the autonomous system network topology", *SIGCOMM Comput. Commun. Rev.*, vol. 31, no. 3, pp. 26–37, ACM, 2001.

[MAQ 96] MAQUELIN O., GAO G. R., HUM H. H. J., THEOBALD K. B. and TIAN X.-M., "Polling watchdog: combining polling and interrupts for efficient message handling", *ISCA*, pp. 179–188, 1996.

[MAR 05a] MARTIN-FLATIN J.-P. and VICAT-BLANC PRIMET P., "Editorial of the special issue high performance networking and services in grids: the dataTAG project", *International Journal of Future Generation Computer System*, vol. 21, no. 4, pp. 439–623, 2005.

[MAR 05b] MARTIN-FLATIN J.-P. and VICAT-BLANC PRIMET P., "Special issue high performance networking and services in grids: the dataTAG project", *International Journal of Future Generation Computer System*, vol. 21, no. 4, pp. 439–623, 2005.

[MAS 04] MASSIE M. L., CHUN B. N. and CULLER D. E., "The ganglia distributed monitoring system: design, implementation, and experience", *Parallel Computing*, vol. 30, no. 5-6, pp. 817–840, 2004.

[MAT 97] MATHIS M., SEMKE J., MAHDAVI J. and OTT T., "The macroscopic behavior of the TCP congestion avoidance algorithm", *Computer Communication Review*, vol. 27, no. 3, 1997.

[MAT 03] MATHIS M., HEFFNER J. and REDDY R., "Web100: extended TCP instrumentation for research, education and diagnosis", *SIGCOMM Comput. Commun. Rev.*, vol. 33, no. 3, pp. 69–79, 2003.

[MIL 00] MILLER N. and STEENKISTE P., "Collecting network status information for network-aware applications", *INFOCOM (2)*, pp. 641–650, 2000.

[MOS 06] MOSKOWITZ R. and NIKANDER P., "Host identity protocol (HIP) architecture", *IETF Request for Comments, RFC 4423*, May 2006.

[NAG 84] NAGLE J., "Congestion control in IP/TCP internetworks", *SIGCOMM*, vol. 14, no. 4, 1984.

[NIK 99] NIKANDER P., An Architecture for Authorization and Delegation in Distributed Object-Oriented Agent Systems, PhD Dissertation, Helsinki University of Technology, April 1999.

[NIK 03] NIKANDER P. and ARKKO J., "Delegation of signalling rights", *Proceedings of the 10th Intl. Workshop on Security Protocols*, Cambridge, UK, April 2003.

[NOR 03] NORD M., BJORNSTAD S. and GAUGER C., "OPS or OBS in the core network", *Proceedings of the 7th IFIP Working Conference on Optical Network Design & Modeling*, 2003.

[NTT 09] 14 Tbps over a Single Optical Fiber: Successful Demonstration of World's Largest Capacity, Press release, July 2009, http://www.ntt.co.jp/news/news06e/0609/060929a.html.

[OUS 96] OUSTERHOUT J. K., "Why threads are a bad idea (for most purposes)?", *USENIX Technical Conference*, January 1996.

[PAD 98a] PADHYE J., FIROIU V., TOWSLEY D. and KUROSE J., "Modeling TCP throughput: a simple model and its empirical validation", *ACM SIGCOMM '98*, 1998.

[PAD 98b] PADMANABHAN V. and KATZ R., "TCP fast start: a technique for speeding up web transfers", *GLOBECOM*, 1998.

[PAX 98a] PAXSON V., ALMES G., MAHDAVI J. and MATHIS M., Framework for IP Performance Metrics, RFC no. 2330, IETF, May 1998.

[PAX 98b] PAXSON V., ALMES G., MAHDAVI J. and MATHIS M., Framework for IP performance metrics, RFC 2330 (Informational), 1998.

[PAX 98c] PAXSON V., MAHDAVI J., ADAMS A. and MATHIS M., "An architecture for large-scale Internet measurement", *IEEE Communications*, vol. 36, no. 8, pp. 48–54, 1998.

[PET 03] PETRINI F., FRACHTENBERG E., HOISIE A. and COLL S., "Performance evaluation of the quadrics interconnection network", *Journal of Cluster Computing*, vol. 6, no. 2, pp. 125–142, 2003.

[PFI 01] PFISTER G. F., "Aspects of the infiniBand™ architecture", *Proceedings of the 2001 IEEE International Conference on Cluster Computing*, Newport Beach, CA, pp. 369–371, October 2001.

[POS 80] POSTEL J., User datagram protocol, RFC 768, August 1980.

[PRI 02] PRIMET P. and HARAKALY R., "Experiment of the NWS (network weather service) network forecasting for Grid Networking", IEEE (Ed.), *Proceedings the Proceedings of the IEEE Conference on Cluster Computing and Grid2002*, Berlin, June 2002.

[PRO 11] PROJECT T., http://www.teragrid.org, 2011.

[PRY 97] PRYLLI L. and TOURANCHEAU B., Protocol design for high performance networking: a myrinet experience, Technical Report 97-22, LIP-ENS Lyon, 69364 Lyon, France, 1997.

[QIA 99] QIAO C. and YOO M., "Optical burst switching-a new paradigm for an optical Internet", *Journal on High-Speed Networks*, vol. 8, no. 1, pp. 69–84, 1999.

[RAM 99] RAMAKRISHNAN K. and FLOYD S., A proposal to add Explicit Congestion Notification (ECN) to IP, RFC no. 2481, IETF, June 1999.

[RAS 07] RASHTI M. J. and AFSAHI A., "10-gigabit iWARP ethernet: comparative performance analysis with infiniBand and myrinet-10G", *Proceedings of the International Workshop on Communication Architecture for Clusters (CAC)*, Long Beach, CA, p. 234, March 2007.

[RHE 05] RHEE I. and XU L., "CUBIC: a new TCP-friendly high-speed TCP variants", *PFLDnet*, February 2005.

[SAL 75] SALTZER J. H. and SCHROEDER M. D., "The protection of information in computer systems", *Proceedings of the IEEE*, vol. 63, no. 9, pp. 1278–1308, 1975.

[SAN 05] SANDER V., "Networking issues for grid infrastructure", *Informational*, June 2005.

[SAR 06] SAROLAHTI P., ALLMAN M. and FLOYD S., "Determining an appropriate sending rate over an underutilized network path", *Computer Networks*, vol. 51, no. 7, pp. 1815–1832, 2006.

[SHO 04] SHORTEN R. and LEITH D., "H-TCP: TCP for high-speed and long-distance networks", *International Conference on Protocols for very Long Distance (PFLDnet'0')*, Argonne, Illinois, USA, February 2004.

[SIT 09] TOP500 SUPERCOMPUTING SITES, http://top500.org, 2009.

[SIV 00] SIVAKUMAR H., BAILEY S. and GROSSMAN R., "PSockets: the case for application-level network stripping for data intensivve applications using high speed wide area networks", *SuperComputing*, November 2000.

[SOU 09a] SOUDAN S., Bandwidth sharing and control in high-speed networks: combining packet- and circuit-switching paradigms, PhD thesis, ENS-Lyon, University of Lyon, France, 2009.

[SOU 09b] SOUDAN S., CHEN B. and VICAT-BLANC PRIMET P., "Flow scheduling and endpoint rate control in GridNetworks", *International Journal of Future Generation Computer Systems (FGCS)*, vol. 25, no. 8, pp. 904–911, 2009.

[SPE 99] SPEIGHT E., ABDEL-SHAFI H. and BENNETT J. K., "Realizing the performance potential of the virtual interface architecture", *International Conference on Supercomputing*, pp. 184–192, 1999.

[SPI 09] SPINNATO P., VICAT-BLANC PRIMET P., EDWARDS C. and WELZL M., "Editorial: special section on networks for grid applications", *International Journal on Future Generation Computer Systems (FGCS)*, vol. 25, no. 8, 2009.

[STE 95] STERLING T., SAVARESE D., BECKER D. J., DORBAND J. E., RANAWAKE U. A. and PACKER C. V., "BEOWULF: a parallel workstation for scientific computation", *Proceedings of the 24th International Conference on Parallel Processing*, Oconomowoc, WI, pp. 11–14, 1995.

[STE 05] STEPHAN E., IP performance metrics (IPPM) metrics registry, RFC 4148 (Best Current Practice), August 2005.

[STO 01] STOCKINGER H., "Distributed database management systems and the data grid", *18th IEEE Symposium on Mass Storage Systems and 9th NASA Goddard Conference on Mass Storage Systems and Technologies*, San Diego, USA, April 17-20 2001.

[SWA 05] SWALLOW G., DRAKE J., ISHIMATSU H. and REKHTER Y., Generalized multiprotocol label switching (GMPLS) user-network interface (UNI): Resource ReserVation Protocol-Traffic Engineering (RSVP-TE) Support for the Overlay Model, RFC 4208 (Proposed Standard), October 2005.

[TAN 06] TAN K., SONG J., ZHANG Q. and SRIDHARAN M., "A compound TCP approach for high-speed and long distance networks", *IEEE INFOCOM*, Apr. 2006.

[TEZ 98] TEZUKA H., O'CARROLL F., HORI A. and ISHIKAWA Y., "Pin-down cache: a virtual memory management technique for zero-copy communication", *Proceedings of the 12th International Parallel Processing Symposium*, pp. 308–315, April 1998.

[VAR 97] VARVARIGOS E. A. and SHARMA V., "The ready-to-go virtual circuit protocol: a loss-free protocol for multigigabit networks using FIFO buffers", *IEEE/ACM Trans. Netw.*, vol. 5, no. 5, pp. 705–718, IEEE Press, 1997.

[VAS 09] VASSEUR J. and ROUX J. L., Path computation element (PCE) communication protocol (PCEP), RFC 5440 (Proposed Standard), March 2009.

[VAZ 01] VAZDKUDAI S., TUECKE S. and FOSTER I., "Replica selection in the globus data grid", PRESS I. C. S. (Ed.), *Proceedings of the First IEEE/ACM International Conference on Cluster Computing and the Grid (CCGRID 2001)*, pp. 106–113, May 2001.

[VER 07] VERDI F., MAGALHÃES M., CARDOZO E., MADEIRA E. and WELIN A., "A service oriented architecture-based approach for interdomain optical network services", *Journal of Network and Systems Management*, vol. 15, no. 2, pp. 141–170, ACM, 2007.

[VIC 02] VICAT-BLANC PRIMET P., ROMIER G. and SOBERMAN M., "Le projet e-toile: développement et mise en oeuvre d'une grille haute performance", *Proceedings of "Journees Nationales du RNTL 2002"*, 2002.

[VIC 05a] VICAT-BLANC PRIMET P., ECHANTILLAC F. and GOUTELLE M., "Experiments of the equivalent differentiated service model in grids", *International Journal Future Generation Computer Systems*, vol. 21, no. 4, pp. 512–524, 2005.

[VIC 05b] VICAT-BLANC PRIMET P., HE E., WELZL M., *et al.*, Survey of protocols other than TCP - GFD 55, Report, Global Grid Forum, April 2005, GFD 55.

[VIC 07] VICAT-BLANC PRIMET P., PASIN M., AUDOUIN O., CHIOSI A., HOUSSIN J.-M., BERDE B., VERCHÈRE D., SOUDAN S., BARTH D., CADÉRÉ C., ECHABBI L., TOMASIK J., REINARD V., VÈQUE V. and ZITOUNE L., Scénarios et besoins réseau pour les applications distribuées, Report, INRIA, July 2007.

[VIC 09a] VICAT-BLANC PRIMET P., GELAS J.-P., MORNARD O., KOSLOVSKI G., ROCA V., GIRAUD L., MONTAGNAT J. and HUU T. T., "A scalable security model for enabling dynamic virtual private execution infrastructures on the Internet", *IEEE International Conference on Cluster Computing and the Grid CCGrid2009*, Shanghai, May 2009.

[VIC 09b] VICAT-BLANC PRIMET P., SOUDAN S. and VERCHERE D., "Virtualizing and scheduling optical network infrastructure for emerging IT services", *Journal of Optical Communications and Networking (JOCN)*, vol. 1, no. 2, pp. A121–A132, 2009.

[WAH 00] WAHEED A., SMITH W., GEORGE J. and YAN J., "An infrastructure for monitoring and management in computational grids", *Languages, Compilers, and Run-Time Systems for Scalable Computers*, vol. 1915/2000 of *Lecture Notes in Computer Science*, pp. 619–628, 2000.

[WEB 08] LAMBDA PROJECT WEBSITE G., http://www.G-LAMBDA.net, October 2008.

[WEI 06] WEI D. X., JIN C., LOW S. H. and HEGDE S., "FAST TCP: motivation, architecture, algorithms, performance", *IEEE/ACM Transactions on Networking*, December 2006.

[WEL 97] WELSH M., BASU A. and VON EICKEN T., "Incorporating memory management into user-level network interfaces", *Proceedings of Hot Interconnects V*, Stanford, August 1997.

[WID 95] WIDJAJA I., "Performance analysis of burst admission-control protocols", *Communications, IEE Proceedings*, vol. 142, no. 1, pp. 7–14, 1995.

[WOL 98] WOLSKI R., "Dynamically forecasting network performance using the Network Weather Service", *Cluster Computing*, vol. 1, no. 1, pp. 119–132, 1998.

[WOL 99] WOLSKI R., SPRING N. and HAYES J., "The network weather service: A distributed resource performance forecasting service for metacomputing", *Future Generation Computing Systems*, vol. 15, pp. 757–768, 1999.

[WU 02] WU J., SAVOIE J. M. and ARNAUD B. S., "Functional requirements of peer-to-peer optical networking", *28th European Conference on Optical Communication*, pp. 1–2, 2002.

[XIA 08] XIAO X., *Technical, Commercial and Regulatory Challenges of QoS: An Internet Service Model Perspective*, Morgan Kaufmann Publishers Inc., San Francisco, CA, USA, 2008.

[XIO 00] XIONG Y., VANDENHOUTE M. and CANKAYA H., "Control architecture in optical burst-switched WDM Networks", *IEEE Journal on Selected Areas in Communications*, vol. 18, no. 10, pp. 1838–1851, 2000.

[XU 04] XU L., HARFOUSH K. and RHEE I., "Binary increase congestion control (BIC) for fast long-distance networks", *INFOCOM 2004: 23rd Annual Joint Conference of the IEEE Computer and Communications Societies*, vol. 4, pp. 2514–2524, 2004.

[YAO 00] YAO S., MUKHERJEE B. and DIXIT S., "Advances in photonic packet switching: an overview", *IEEE Communications Magazine*, vol. 38, no. 2, pp. 84–94, 2000.

[ZAL 09] ZALESKY A., "To burst or circuit switch?", *IEEE/ACM Trans. Netw.*, vol. 17, no. 1, pp. 305–318, IEEE Press, 2009.

Acronyms and Definitions

Throughout this book, we introduce and use acronyms, the main definitions of which we group here:

– Accounting: measurement of resources consumed.

– API: application programming interface.

– ASDL: Asymmetric Digital Subscriber Line.

– ASTN: automatic switched transport networks.

– ATM: asynchronous transfer mode. A cell-switching level 2 network protocol, the objective of which is to multiplex different data streams on the same link using a time multiplexing technique.

– Batch processing: execution of a set of jobs in a non-interactive way (for an example, see PBS).

– BDP: bandwidth delay product. Measurement frequently used for the adjustment of transport control protocol parameters.

– BSS: business support systems. Elements of the architecture that manage products, clients, revenues and commands.

– Certificate policy: named set of rules indicating the possibility of applying for a certificate for a particular community and/or a class of applications with common security needs.

– Certification authority (CA): the authority trusted by one or more users to create and issue certificates. The certification authority can create user keys.

– Computing element: abstraction representing a computer cluster in a grid. It is identified by a list of computing nodes (IP address and port). In the Globus system, a local resource manager and a GateKeeper for access control (GRAM) correspond to each computing element.

– Cluster: set (group) of machines (nodes) interconnected to share heavy processing; often one server node (master) is designated to be in charge of distributing work on the client nodes.

– Cloud: cloud computing or dematerialized computing is a concept that makes reference to providing computing services across the Internet. This concept has three levels:

- infrastructure as a service (IaaS), which enables use of computing memory, capacities of computers and servers distributed across the world;

- platform as a service (PaaS) for the use of remote software production tools; and

- software as a service (SaaS) for applications.

– Computing grid: group of resources, especially computing, geographically and organizationally disseminated ones giving users the possibility to execute applications on a subset of theses resources, in a transparent way.

– Data confidentiality: this service can be used to protect data against non-authorized divulging of information. The data confidentiality service is supported by the authentification framework. It can be used to protect data against interception.

– Delegation: transfer of a privilege from an entity that has the privilege to another entity.

– DLL: dynamically linked library. This is a library that is dynamically linked to the code that makes use of it: the set of routines (modules or sub-programs) extracted from a main program, to be shared by several programs or to optimize memory occupation (DLLs that can be charged and discharged at will).

– DMZ: demilitarized zone, neutral zone.

– DNS: Domain Name Service. This is a hierarchical service that converts symbolic names into machine addresses on a network (IP address); for example the name www.foo.fr is transformed into IP address 192.54.193.134.

– DSM: distributed shared memory enables distributed processes to exchange information by giving the illusion of having memory that is common to all.

– EGEE: Enabling Grids for E-sciencE.

– Encryption system: a set of transformations to obtain an encrypted text and, reciprocally, the choice of the particular transformation(s) to use. Transformations are generally defined by a mathematical algorithm.

– Environment variables: these are the characteristics of a policy necessary for an authorization decision. Such variables are not contained in static structures but are locally accessible by a privileged entity (for example, the day and time or the current account).

– FCAPS: Fault, Configuration, Accounting, Performance, Security. This is a management model for telecommunications networks.

– GIIS: Grid Index Information Service. This is the information service in Globus.

– Globus: the open source *de facto* standard grid middleware, proposed by Argonne laboratories (United States).

– Globus Toolkit: this contains all of the grid tools proposed by Globus.

– Grid infrastructure: grid platform(s), associated with engineering and implementation ensuring its (their) functioning at the expected quality.

– GridFTP: FTP services for a computing grid implementing several parallel transport control protocol flows.

– GMPLS: generalized multi protocol label switching. Transport networks unified control plan.

– Grid node: a set of persistent processes and memory spaces. Generally, a PC or a server is considered as a node in a server cluster for high-performance grids. It often corresponds to a geographical localization.

– Grid platform: aggregation of network nodes and links managed by a specialized middleware with corresponding monitoring, administration, security, etc., utilities.

– Grid service: processing offered by a grid to its users and to user applications of a high level (resource management, job monitoring) as well as of the lowest level (message exchange, file transfer, etc.). Web services defined by the W3 consortium ensure Open Grid Services Architecture (OGSA) standards and Open Grid Services Infrastructure or OGSI (callable protocols and services) are met. These services can also be called Service Oriented Architecture (in the sense of web services) directly by application programming interfaces).

– GSI: Grid Security Infrastructure. Sub-system of Globus middleware.

– Heartbeat monitor: module for auditing distributed processes that have been declared by a service.

– Holder: an entity that has received delegation of a privilege, either directly from the source of authority or indirectly through another attribute authority.

– HTML: HyperText Markup Language. The webpage description language.

– HTTP: the HyperText Transfer Protocol is a hypertext data-transmission protocol used in the framework of the web to transmit pages and their contents (images, sounds, etc.).

– IETF: the Internet Engineering Task Force is the committee helping to define and develop the Internet and applications that use it.

– ISP: Internet service provider.

– Job: application or independent coherent subset of applications, accompanied by the description of services requested of the grid and their sequencing.

– Load balancing: distribution of resource needs over all available means.

– Middleware: set of software layers forming an administration, monitoring, operating, management system of a set of components that can be managed via interfaces by human operators or applications.

– IP: the Internet Protocol is a packet-oriented data-transport protocol used on the Internet to mask the heterogeneity of interconnected networks.

– IPPM: IP performance metrics. Designates metrics to the Internet Engineering Task Force that standardizes concepts linked to performance measurement of an IP network.

– ISO: the International Standardization Organization, which, for example, established a layer model for data exchange in networks.

– ITU: The International Telecommunication Union is an organization that contributes to standards, for example on telecommunication networks and distributed systems.

– Job: a managed elementary execution entity. It is a set of related processes, run as a whole. A job can often be seen as a shell script. In POSIX terminology, a job is a group of sessions. A session is a group of interdependent processes.

– LDAP: the Lightweight Directory Access Protocol is a network protocol of the X500 type. It is designed for operating in TCP/IP stacks to extract information from a hierarchical directory such as X500. It offers the user a unique tool for finding information in a set of data, such as a user name, an e-mail address, a security certificate, etc.

– LSP: label switched paths.

– MDS: the Monitoring and Discovery Service is a Globus service that was formerly called the Metacomputing Directory Service; its role was redefined and re-centered as an Information Service Protocol.

– Message-passing: a process of communication between processes through which information is exchanged via message-sending, whether asynchronous or not, in contrast, for example, with communication by shared memory; see MPI.

– Metadata: piece of information relating to data, for example by giving a description or properties.

– Middleware: this layer is in charge of exchanging information between distributed processes, masking the heterogeneity of machines and underlying networks by as much as possible.

– MPI: The Message-Passing Interface is commonly used in parallel message-passing systems. It is faster than PVM (Parallel Virtual Machine) but less portable.

– MTBF: mean time before failure.

– MTTR: mean time to repair is the unavailability time that corresponds to the period elapsed between the occurrence of a failure and re-opening of the system.

– MTU: maximum transfer unit.

– Multicast: broadcast of packets to groups of receivers.

– NAT: network address translation, the principal function is to share a given public IP among several users using private IPs.

– OADM: optical add-drop multiplexers. Device composed of two different types of optical add ports, and two of the same types of optical drop ports, the function of which is to add or drop wavelengths.

– OBS: optical burst switching.

– OCS: optical circuit switching.

– OGSA: Open Grid Services Architecture.

– OGSI: Open Grid Services Infrastructure.

– OPS: optical packet switching.

– OS: operating system. Low-layer software that allows to expose and share the resources of a computing system so that they can be used by programs.

– OSI: the Open Systems Interconnection model is a communication standard for the interconnection of open systems, defined by the International Standardization Organization.

– OSS: operational support systems. Elements of the architecture that take care of aspects of management for a telecommunications service provider.

– OXC: optical cross-connect. Optical equipment that enables network operators to interconnect fibers and control the communication of wavelengths in the network.

– PBS: Portable Batch System. Very popular system of job-management in batches.

– PCE: path computation element (RFC 4655). The path-computation service in a network.

– P2P: peer-to-peer. Distributed programming principle in which all entities have equivalent roles.

– Ping: the name of a command enabling an Internet Control Message Protocol echo request to be sent from one machine to another. If the end machine does not respond, it cannot be communicated with.

– PKI: the public key infrastructure is an organizational and technical framework that makes use of certificates based on public key cryptography. It enables management of the said certificates by offering security services aimed at a set of users and applications in a public or private network. PKI provides authentification, encryption, integrity and non-repudiation services.

– POP: point of presence: end-point of an Internet backbone.

– Private key: the key in a user's pair of keys that is known solely to the user.

– Process: local unit of execution on a computer in the UNIX sense. A job launches the creation and execution of a process.

– Public key: the key in a user's pair of keys that is publicly known in an encryption system.

– Public key certificate: the public key of a user, associated with some other information that has been made non-falsifiable by encryption using the private key of the sending certification authority.

– Public Key Infrastructure: see PKI.

– QoS: quality of service. Defines guarantees of the level of service in terms of delay, response time, throughput and reliability.

– RDF: Resource Description Framework.

– Resource: typical elements made available by the grid. We distinguish between application resources provided between applications (executables, files, etc.) and system resources belonging to the grid (processors, elements of memory, network elements, etc.). We also distinguish software resources from hardware resources. All resources are described in a repertoire made up of a catalog of metadata and the dynamic status of all grid resources.

– Resource manager or resource broker: component of a computing grid that is in charge of resource allocation to applications requesting them, thus carrying out load-balancing on the grid. This component can be centralized.

– RMI: remote method invocation. This is a mechanism that enables Java object methods located on another virtual machine (distributed objects) to be called, whether they are on the same computer or on another machine accessible by the network.

– RPC: the Remote Procedure Call is synchronous remote invocation method suggested by Sun.

– RTT: round trip time. This is the round trip delay of a packet between two points of a network.

– Service broker: component of middleware in charge of the management of all system resources, relying on a repertoire of such resources described in the form of metadata (designation, description and properties of the resource) and on their status.

– SACK: selective acknowledgment. This is selective acquittal used by Transport Control Protocol.

– SOA: Service Oriented Architecture (in the sense of web services).

– SOAP: Simple Object Access Protocol. This is a protocol managing the rules related to data representation (numbers, tables, etc.) and processing to enable the possibility of enriching the types and formats of recognized data.

– SSL: the Secure Socket Layer is a standard transparent data-encryption process. It is a protocol that enables mutual authentification between a client and a server and establishes an authentificated and encrypted connection.

– Task: local subunit of the execution of a process.

– TCP: Transport Control Protocol. This is a data-transport protocol relying on IP but ensuring the correction of data flow sent (recovery of lost packets, ensuring of packet-integrity, desequencing correction, etc.).

– Traceroute: this is a utility program that enables us to follow the path a data packet (IP packet) will take to go from the local machine to another machine connected to the network.

– UDDI: Universal Description, Discovery and Integration. This is a joined norm based on Web Services Description Language (WSDL) and proposed by 55 companies (including Microsoft, IBM, Ariba and HP). It aims to create directories of B2B web services by profession. Each company can subscribe to it, register the web services it proposes and describe how its partners can be electronically integrated to carry out B2B transactions. These directories include:

   - the green pages: implementation details necessary for integration of service;

   - white pages: general information on the company proposing the service; and

   - yellow pages: information on the company's profession.

– UDP: the User Datagram Protocol is light protocol on top of IP ensuring a simple and fast transport service.

– UML: Unified Modeling Language. Object modeling and notation graphic language object defined by the Object Management Group to visualize, specify, construct and document events intervening in a distributed system of objects.

– URI: the Uniform Resource Identifier is a global resource identification system consisting of a chain of characters in arborescence that enable a service and associated resources to be called. The shape of the arborescence is defined in a diagram, such as that presented by the W3C.

– URL: the Uniform Resource Locator is an object addressing system accessible from the web (access address and protocol).

– User account: representation of laws and a point where information related to the use of grid resources by a user or a group of users is attached (independently or not of a Virtual Organization).

– UUID: the universally unique identifier is generally on eight bytes, is randomly generated and considered to be unique. For example, 2b9e2e24-60e8-4801- a384-d4ce1919ea1a is a UUID created by uuidgen.

– Virtual Organization: definition of an organization of resources and grid users, with subsets of resources on the grid system at the disposal of users linked to this virtual organization. Also called VO.

– VLAN: Virtual Local Area Network. For more information, see IEEE standard 802.1Q.

– VO: see Virtual Organization.

– W3C: the WorldWide Web Consortium is a web standardization committee (for example: HTML, XML, SOAP, etc.)

– WDM: wavelength-division multiplexing includes methods used to transport several different optical signals on a single fiber.

– Web service: a set of norms enabling access to applications via a declaration of services offered by these and a standardized set of protocols:
      - SOAP (Single Access Object Protocol),
      - UDDI (Universal Description, Discovery and Integration),
      - WSDL (Web Services Description Language),
      - XML (eXtended Markup Language).

– Web Services: processing units put at the disposal of third parties in a web context.

– WSDL: the Web Services Description Language is a format based on XML that enables the functionalities of a service to be exposed to the world outside. It gives information about accepted parameters and the nature of the service rendered.

– XML: eXtensible Markup Language is the descriptive language of beacon bases. It is a metalanguage (a set of generic rules) used to describe a markup language.

– XSL: eXtensible Stylesheet Language is an XML (an XSL style sheet is an XML document) application (a derived language). In practice, XSL is a language used to manipulate XML documents. It is the equivalent of CSS-style sheets for HTML. XSL enables us to define how the support (webpage, mobile screen, printed page, etc.) must publish and restore the associated XML document. This enables separation between data structures (XML) and restoration (XSL).

Index